THE RUTHLESS NORTHLAKE BANK ROBBERS

A 1967 SHOOTING SPREE THAT STUNNED THE REGION

EDGAR GAMBOA NÁVAR

THE History PRESS

Published by The History Press
Charleston, SC
www.historypress.net

First published 2016

Manufactured in the United States

ISBN 978.1.46711.938.2

Library of Congress Control Number: 2016930886

To my mom and dad,
for their love

CONTENTS

PREFACE

Northlake, Illinois, a Chicago suburb, is Cook County's most western suburb. Near Northlake's water tower sits a small park. In that park, you find swings, an in-ground water fountain for young children to play in and a kiosk with benches underneath. The park is very well kept and serves community members of all ages. That was the park's initial intent: to serve as a reminder of the servant-minded police officers who are that park's namesake.

Nagle-Perri Park was named after two police officers who were killed during a bank robbery in 1967. It wasn't just any bank robbery. It was a famous bank robbery—a bank robbery that grabbed the attention of our country's leaders for several reasons. One reason was the brutal nature of the officers' death. The officers' guns did not compare to the thieves' military assault weapons. A second reason was that the robbers were repeat offenders who had fulfilled prison requirements. They were considered rehabilitated prisoners. The final reason was that the tumultuous decade of the 1960s questioned the constitutionality of capital punishment. So, three bank robbers, their actions and their capture were temporarily propelled onto the national scene.

As a high school student, I enjoyed the park's basketball court. My friends and I gathered there frequently to play ball. After games we often walked past the American flag that had a rock at its base. On that rock was a plaque that commemorated two police officers. One specific day, I read the plaque and inquired of my friends about the two police officers. They told me their

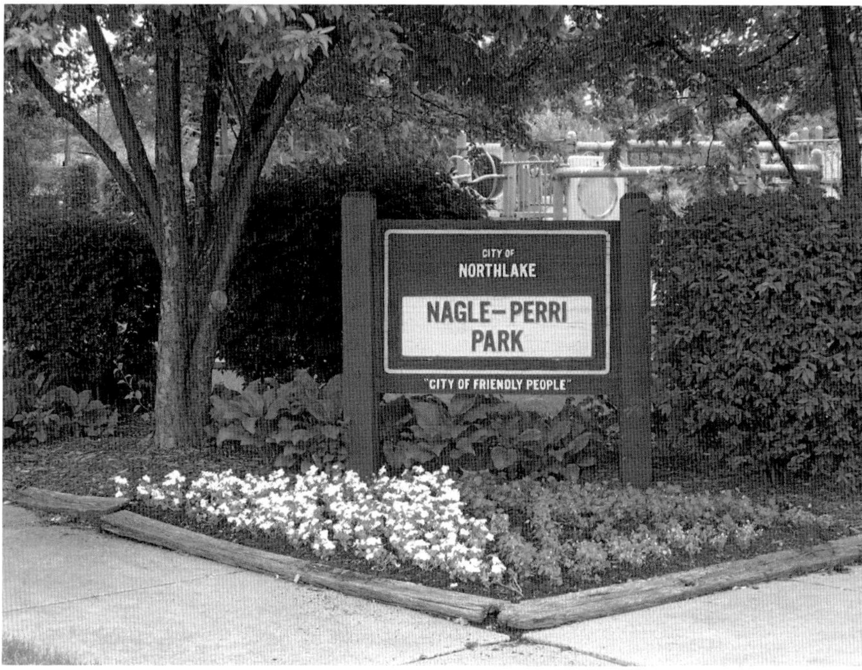

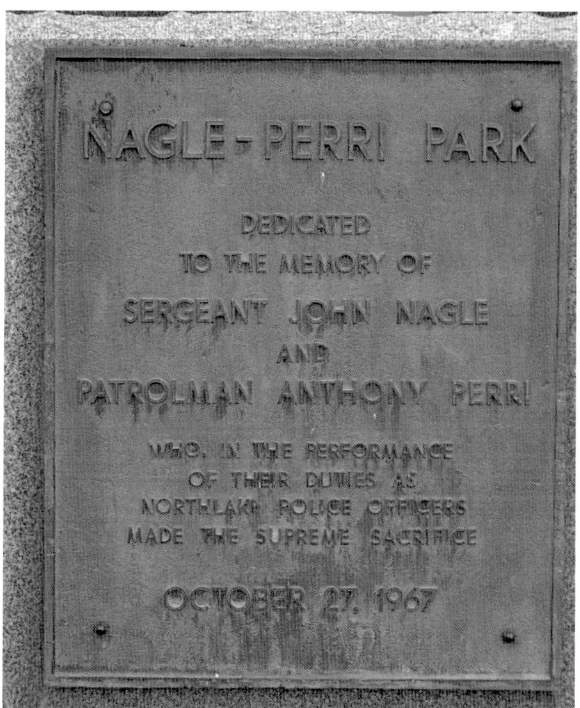

Above: The main sign to Northlake's Nagle-Perri Park, which sits on the corner of Roy Avenue and Parkview Drive under the town's water tower. *Photo taken by Edgar Gamboa Návar.*

Left: A plaque in Northlake's Nagle-Perri Park that commemorates the lives of the two fallen Northlake police officers John Nagle and Anthony Perri. *Photo taken by Edgar Gamboa Návar.*

story. I was quickly intrigued since the bank robbery occurred near my backyard. I carried that story for years afterward.

Over the years, as residents talked and discussed the bank robbery, my intrigue grew. In early 2011, I researched the bank robbery and the events that surrounded it. The more I learned, the more interesting the events of that day became in my mind. I put pen to paper and started my project.

In many ways, the events of October 27, 1967, represented so much more than just a bank robbery. The events represented migration, suburbs birthing and expanding to meet demand and new opportunities for many new residents. The dynamics of that event represented socioeconomic and shifting cultural attitudes on a national landscape.

The story cannot be told without realizing that the families of one offender and one murdered police officer grew up near Chicago's Little Italy. I couldn't help but think of times when perhaps their parents passed one another on the way to the Italian markets to buy groceries, or perhaps they had mutual acquaintances. Decades later, one set of parents' son fired bullets into the body of another set of parents' son, murdering him.

Even after the shooting, parallel events emerged. As the family of one officer gathered in his home to mourn his loss, the culprits were housed in the second-floor apartment of a nearby home, ready to die in a shootout if police approached.

I took every quote in this narrative from newspaper accounts, FBI reports or other official documents, such as court transcripts. I attempted to stick close to the actual events of this story with the goal of letting the story tell itself. Like any good and true story, I did not embellish or change the facts. A good story tells itself. My goal was to have the story's events drive the narrative. I hope I have accomplished that task.

Chapter 1

REHABILITATED PRISONERS

On Wednesday, November 2, 1967, FBI director J. Edgar Hoover spoke at the FBI National Academy's graduation ceremony for law enforcement officers. Hoover stated, "I believe in parole, but I do not believe in the sloppy method in which it is administered at both the federal and local levels. There is need for correction of it by Congress and by the local communities to support the local law enforcement officers and the decent citizens of the community."[1] Hoover assailed the nation's parole system, specifically mentioning two police-slaying Northlake, Illinois bank robbers who had been granted parole earlier that year from a federal prison. Hoover remarked, "I'm glad to say this morning that the two men who murdered the two Chicago police officers this past week were apprehended last night."[2] Hoover desired to return to the fundamentals of law enforcement and the proper administration of the parole system. Law and order was essential to provide safety for the country's citizens.

Preceding Hoover, the ceremony's two other speakers voiced their opinions. Los Angeles police chief Thomas Reddin shared his thoughts: "The ancient Greek philosophers agreed that there was one constant thing in the Universe and that was constant change…change is one of the greatest problems facing the law enforcement scene."[3] Reddin continued, "We have rapid—almost daily—changes in social, economic, and philosophical values…as a nation, we are having a problem deciding what group and which philosophy will prevail for over 200 million people in this country."[4] Reddin saw societal shifts in attitudes that affected law and order: criminals were to be punished.

Reddin's speech further stated that too much crime had been excused for social disadvantages, such as poor childhoods. "Too much crime is condoned on the flimsy excuse that a poor childhood and society's failure cause crime and thus constitute a license to rob and to riot."[5] "I don't believe society causes crime. People cause crime. And if a poor childhood were the automatic road to ruin, many in this audience would be in jail rather than here today."[6] Reddin saw firsthand the amount of excusable crime that supposedly stemmed from social disadvantages in Los Angeles. To excuse those crimes was naïve and irresponsible.

The ceremony's other speaker, J. Howard Wood, the *Chicago Tribune*'s publisher, also commented on the surging national debate. Wood stated, "Without law and order there can be no economic progress, no social progress, and indeed, nothing but chaos…violence, crime, and mob rule never advanced anybody's cause or anybody's country."[7] Admitting his departure from the prepared comments, Wood then remarked, "I was informed that the two desperados who were picked up on the charge of killing those two fine police officers in the bank robbery in Northlake were recently paroled men."[8]

Wood then cited his disagreement with the restrictions on disclosure. He stated, "The advocates of restraint, besides displaying lack of faith in judges and juries, are also equally guilty of showing a complete lack of confidence in the judgment, integrity, and good sense of the police and, of course, the press itself."[9] Wood believed that police and the press could "freely exchange information and inform the public," while the "defendant can still have a fair day in court."[10] For Wood, the newspapers assisted law enforcement in capturing criminals by disseminating critical information to the public.

Wood differed with bar and judiciary committees that argued to restrict disclosure of information about pending criminal cases. The principal argument lay on defendants' rights to a fair trial that are potentially prejudiced as a result of information disclosure regarding the pending case. In other words, the defendant might not receive a fair trial if too much information is leaked. The topic of a defendant's rights versus having proper case information to make a decision was key. The national media attention that the Northlake Bank robbers received propelled that case to the forefront from both the law enforcement angle and from the media outlets.

THE NATIONAL DEBATE concerning parole raged. Prison inmates were punished for their actions. Wrongs were to be righted. Perpetrators faced consequences for their actions. However, parole boards' desires were for rehabilitated prisoners. Prisoners' social situations contributed to their misbehavior. Too many prisoners were uneducated, skill-less and without future hope. Prisons intended to provide avenues for reform with the hope that rehabilitated prisoners would reintegrate themselves into society.

Immediately following the stinging comments at the FBI graduation ceremony, the recently appointed U.S. Parole Board chairman, Walter Dunbar, gave his own assessment with regard to the Northlake Bank robbers. Dunbar studied both Clifton Orneal Daniels's and Henry Michael Gargano's files. Dunbar gave his own analysis, stating that he, too, would have granted both men parole. That decision would have been based on both men's prison accomplishments and personal backgrounds. Both men made "basic adjustments in their lives, completed high school in prison, and successfully took college level courses."[11] Dunbar quickly retorted to Hoover's statement: "It's easy to see if a prisoner has had his teeth fixed in prison or has learned to tune an engine, but when we get into areas of how to measure his attitude, what he'll do when he gets out, how he'll react to his associates, these are less precise."[12] For Dunbar, forming successful parolees was a less-than-perfect science.

Chicago's chief of parole for the District of Illinois, Ben Meeker, made statements that agreed with Dunbar. The families of both men "were convinced that they were going straight since they were freed from prison."[13] Meeker commented that "there was nothing about these men to indicate any kind of crisis which required closer observation."[14] Gargano was trained as a plumber, while Daniels was trained as a dental technician. Both Dunbar and Meeker desired to know the frequency of each prisoner's meetings with their parole officers. Something had gone gravely wrong in the parole of Daniels and Gargano from the government's most secured maximum institution. The parole board's mission was to maintain that fine balance of not having overcrowded prisons yet releasing rehabilitated prisoners back into society.

Prison term reductions in the United States date back to 1867. The first statute regarding reduction as a result of good behavior was enacted that year. With consent of the local officials, such as the prison warden, "a deduction was made of one month in each year from the term of sentence of federal prisoners confined in state jails or penitentiaries."[15] Three years later, the Department of Justice was formed, and it amended the 1867 act to institutions where no system of good credits applied. By 1891, the attorney general had the authority to reduce sentences. Eleven years later, in 1902, the decision was made to have good time credits increase with length of sentence. However, the power resided with each prison's local officials to grant good credits.

The federal parole system was officially started in 1910. A prisoner was eligible for parole after completing one-third of his sentence. The board of parole consisted of the superintendent of the Department of Justice, the warden and the physician of the local penitentiary. A parole officer was responsible for each parolee—the parole system remained that way for decades.

In 1930, a unified parole system was established. Legislation passed on May 13, 1930, created a single board of parole based in Washington, D.C. The attorney general appointed the three members of the board of parole. By 1950, the required number of board members had increased to eight. The president, with the Senate's approval, appointed all eight board members.

In 1966, the U.S. Board of Parole ruled on 13,844 cases. Ronald Dale Raine was one of those cases. Raine was paroled in June 1966. The following year, 1967, the U.S. Board of Parole officially granted parole to Clifton Orneal Daniels on January 9 and to Henry Michael Gargano on March 20, both from Marion Federal Penitentiary in Illinois. And so it was that the federal parole board considered all three federal prisoners rehabilitated, releasing them after serving less than half of their prison terms.

Origins: Henry Michael Gargano

Henry Michael Gargano was born to Anthony Gargano and Emma Rinck in Chicago's Cook County Hospital on January 25, 1932. A few blocks from the hospital was their home, at 821 South Ashland Avenue, near Polk Street, and just a mile away was Chicago's famous Little Italy neighborhood, the heart of Italian immigration. Chicago's Little Italy was home to more than seventy thousand foreign-born Italians in 1930, many of them poor. Although Italian culture reigned supreme, Anthony and Emma Gargano lived in an area where poor living conditions existed for many Italians. At age twenty-nine, the year Henry was born, Anthony Gargano worked as a shipping clerk for the Sawyer Biscuit Company, a job he had held for the previous six years to support his twenty-eight-year-old wife and two sons.

The Sawyer Biscuit Company was located on the city's Near West Side, on Harrison Street, just west of Halsted. Famously known in the Midwest, Sawyer crackers carried the moniker "The Best Crackers on Earth." In the late 1920s, the Sawyer Biscuit Company was one of several cracker bakeries that merged to form United Biscuit, which was headquartered in Chicago. After the merger, the Sawyer bakery employed about 350 persons throughout the 1930s.[16] Anthony Gargano was one of those 350 employees. Anthony's wife, Emma, would spend her days primarily working in the home as a housewife. Emma Gargano's maiden name was Rinck. Her father, Adolph Rinck, owned a cottage in northern Indiana, near Upper Fish Lake. Adolph Rinck's cottage eventually played a prominent role decades later in his grandson Henry's life.

GARGANO'S EARLY LIFE was filled with trouble. His first known crime took place when he was fourteen years of age. Gargano's family moved west two miles from his birthplace on Ashland Avenue in Chicago to a place near California Avenue. At age fourteen, Gargano and a boyhood friend, William Hart, were given a dollar to wheel 136 pounds of stolen butter to a vacant garage near Twenty-eighth and Lexington. The butter was stolen from a Central Grocers Cooperative in nearby Oak Park. Although Gargano and his childhood friend did not commit the original crime, they accepted payment to wheel the stolen butter. As both boys wheeled it down an alleyway, a detective noticed them, stopped them and took both boys into the station for questioning. Gargano and Hart were both sent to juvenile authorities.

Both boys were arraigned before Judge Frank Bicek in juvenile court and were charged with the theft of 136 pounds of butter. Unfortunately for both of them, butter was not the only theft the company suffered—four thousand sticks of gum had also been stolen. Although neither Gargano nor Hart participated in the gum theft, Judge Bicek pressed for the two boys to admit to their participation, and Gargano and Hart both yielded to the pressure and said they had committed the crime. Unlike Hart, whose father was present during the court date, Gargano's father was absent due to illness. In some ways, Gargano was his own man. During his teenage years, Gargano's mother was the sole provider. Gargano was eventually sent to Illinois State Training School for Boys in St. Charles, Illinois, about a two-hour drive from his Chicago home.

Originally called the St. Charles School and Home for Boys, the Illinois State Training School for Boys opened in December 1904. The complex sat on over nine hundred acres of farmland. Similar to the parole program the

Northlake Bank robbers were beneficiaries of, this school and home for boys intended to provide young male offenders with intellectual and vocational skills so they could be useful to society. That was the intended purpose for Gargano: to live in the cottage-style homes with the goal of developing intellectual and vocational skills.

Although Gargano spent time at this training school for boys, he would continually encounter trouble with the law. He was charged multiple times during his juvenile years. Charges included unlawfully driving a vehicle as a minor, larceny and multiple charges for robbery. With the exception of driving the vehicle as a minor, Gargano committed all these crimes in the state of Illinois, the majority of them in the Chicago area.

Authorities eventually charged Gargano multiple times with armed robbery and bank robberies; he spent the majority of his life in jail, serving time in Illinois, Indiana and Pennsylvania. While serving time in a Pennsylvania penitentiary, Gargano established a friendship with a fellow inmate, Ralph Garduno. Years later, they would do a robbery together in Ohio. One of them would be caught and create a trail that would lead to the capture of several men wanted for bank robbery. That relationship was established in prison.

Origins: Ronald Dale Raine

On November 31, 1930, Ronald Dale Raine was born to Ora Earl Raine and Leonora Lela Buzard in Great Falls, Montana, a city about ninety miles from the state capital of Helena. Ronald was the second child born to his parents. His father, originally from Kansas, had moved to Montana decades previously and married Raine's mother, Leonora. Ronald was born to working parents: his mom primarily dedicated herself to housework, and his father was a salesman. Specifically, Ora Earl Raine worked for approximately fifteen years selling farm equipment. Raine's parents had a total of four children: Gene, Merton, Ronald and a daughter, name unknown. Similar to Daniels, Ronald Dale Raine had a farming upbringing, away from any metropolitan center—and away from supposedly vicious crimes that occurred exclusively in metropolises.

The Raine family soon moved to Willow Creek, Montana, near Bozeman. They owned a farm near Cottonwood Canyon, the major source of income for the Raines. Ronald Dale Raine was always energetic, getting himself into local trouble with other area youths. When Raine was a young boy, his father left the family unannounced, leaving Leonora and the four kids alone, never giving them reasons for his departure. They never heard back from him. Ronald Dale Raine and his siblings were greatly impacted by their father's abandonment. Leonora felt the economic pinch. She quickly secured a job as a schoolteacher in Willow Creek, where she taught for three years, from 1941 to 1944. At that time, Leonora moved her family to Selah, Washington, for better economic opportunities. Ronald Dale Raine was fourteen years old. Raine's small-town antics and energetic style rapidly developed into serious crimes. He associated himself with a rough crowd of teenage boys, a lifestyle that took a sharp turn after high school. Raine's mother, however, further immersed herself in education, continuing her profession in their new hometown of Selah.

During high school, Raine was a B and C student. Raine's greatest academic struggles were in math and science, primarily getting C's and D's. Raine took no foreign languages but instead took courses in the industrial arts. Raine did not excel in those courses either. His interests were focused on activities outside school, spending time with a rough crowd. Although his relationships led him to commit theft frequently, Raine did graduate from Selah High School in May 1948, ranking fifty-seventh in his class.

Soon after high school, Raine's association with rough teenage boys became evident. Raine stated, "I decided to try to become a professional thief—it was a quicker way to riches than working."[17] Raine and his friends began stealing cars, driving them to Denver and selling them. That provided quick cash. Raine developed into an expert locksmith, a skill that enabled him to become a talented thief. Raine could study a key for a few moments and duplicate an exact copy minutes later. That skill proved useful when stealing cars.

Raine and his group of friends continued their wily ways. Soon, they wanted more than simply stealing cars. Raine moved on to other thefts to provide even greater exhilaration. The more daring the crime, the more exhilaration ran through his body.

Raine then spent time in the Washington State Monroe Reformatory for a series of armed robberies. He robbed a Tacoma, Washington Safeway store in September 1953 at gunpoint and was arrested and charged for that crime in February 1954. Raine later stated, "Unfortunately, my criminal studies consisted mainly of perusing True and Official Detective type magazines; after all, they're titled 'True and Official,' so they must be so."[18] Raine developed a consistent prison routine throughout his late teenage years and into his twenties—continually in and out of prison. Raine's habit of theft eventually escalated even further, dangerously further. Along with two other men, Ronald Dale Raine found himself in greater trouble on a late October morning in 1967 just outside Chicago.

Origins: Clifton Orneal Daniels

Clifton Orneal Daniels was born on September 12, 1938, in Wayne County to Earl Daniels and Opal Irene Schackleford of Mt. Erie, Illinois. Earl Daniels worked as a farmer, tilling the land, a laborious and tedious task that proved difficult years later for Clifton. Opal, worked as a housewife. She was the mother of four children: Wilma, Glen, Gerald and Clifton.

Clifton Daniels attended school locally—he eventually enrolled at Cisne High School in 1952. Although he started high school in Cisne, Clifton did not graduate from high school there. Years later, through a prison-offered rehabilitation program, Daniels completed the high school requirements. Clifton's life on the farm remained uneventful. He desired a more adventurous life beyond the fields of Cisne. Clifton's life soon became adventure-filled in a misguided and tragic way.

Clifton Daniels, a downstate Illinois resident, also developed a prolific criminal history. Daniels was charged multiple times with crimes: attempt to commit larceny and carrying a concealed weapon. Both of those early charges were in Illinois. Daniels was next charged twice in California, after being stationed there with the navy. He was charged with suspicion of kidnapping, suspicion of robbery and suspicion of automobile theft. However, the charges of robbery and auto theft were dropped due to insufficient evidence. Daniels was then committed to the California Youth Authority (CYA) for an indeterminate sentence on kidnapping in 1958 and was sent to Chino, California. Daniels was then transferred to the Tracy Institute in Tracy, California, from which he was released in February 1960 on parole to the State of Illinois.

After returning to Illinois, Daniels faced more legal challenges. He was fingerprinted for reckless driving on a revoked license in Olney, Illinois, and reckless driving on a suspended license in Vandalia, Illinois. Daniels then changed his brushes with the law into more serious offenses. He was charged with bank robbery and unlawful flight to avoid prosecution for bank robbery in Lexington, Kentucky.

After serving brief prison stints in Illinois, Kansas, Indiana and Pennsylvania for bank robbery, Daniels eventually served time in Illinois in the Marion Penitentiary. His charge was the same as recent previous charges: bank robbery and conspiracy. During his stint in Marion, Daniels established a friendship with another fellow inmate who had served time for bank robbery—Henry Gargano.

Both men went through prison rehabilitation programs provided in Marion. They took high school– and college-level courses. The purpose for these programs was to give prison inmates skills that they could use once they were released from prison. Socially disadvantaged persons such as Gargano and Daniels *supposedly* benefited from these programs. The rationale was that their deviant behavior extended from their personal experiences and background. The theory was that if repeat offenders such as Gargano and Daniels developed skills to reintegrate themselves into society, they would cease their lives of crime. Ironically, Gargano's reform participation in Marion was similar to his initial experiences at the Illinois State Training School for Boys in Saint Charles, Illinois, decades before, when he was a teenage boy. Unfortunately for several Northlake police officers, the rehabilitation program at Marion provided similar results. Gargano returned to his life of crime.

After his release on parole supervision in January 1967, Daniels had brief work stints with U.S. Steel and Des Plaines Chemical Company. On June 5, 1967, Daniels secured a final job with the aid of his former fellow prisoner Henry Gargano. Both men worked for several months at the Centracchio Construction Company, based in Lyons, Illinois. They were dismissed on September 22, 1967.

Origins: Anthony Perri

Less than two miles from Henry Gargano's family's residence, another Italian American family—the Perris—lived in Chicago's Little Italy. Anthony was born to Theodore Perri and Minnie Ferraro of 835 South Loomis on September 16, 1926. Theodore was thirty-four years of age when Anthony was born. Minnie was thirty-one years old at the time of his birth. Theodore, born in Italy, moved to the United States as part of the large Italian migration waves. He now worked as a tailor to support his family. Minnie, on the other hand, was born in Chicago and dedicated herself to rearing eight children as a housewife.

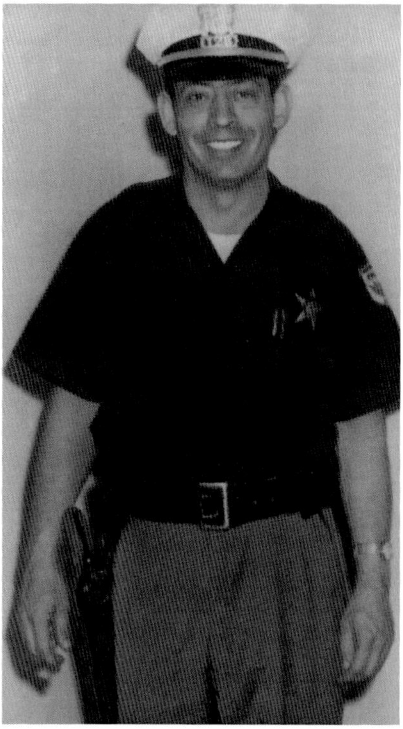

An official Northlake police photo of Anthony Perri. *Courtesy of Northlake Police Department.*

For Theodore, living a few blocks from Taylor Street and Chicago's Little Italy was as close to living back home in Italy as he could get. The language, customs, foods and smells of Italy were prevalent in this part of Chicago. So the Perris raised their eight children as best they could in the late 1920s and 1930s. When Anthony reached school age, the Perris enrolled him in the local public school.

Anthony attended Henry Shepard Elementary School on the 2800 block of Fillmore Street, just south of Taylor Street. He tried, as many kids did, to do well in school. The immigrant standards entrenched in him were no different than those of other kids attending those neighborhood schools. School was important.

In so many ways, the school's namesake remained true to this section of town. Henry Olandorf Shepard was an entrepreneur and businessman at heart. He started in the printing business and later founded Inkland Printer. Shepard was a hard worker. He wasn't too different from a certain student attending those years in the early 1930s: Anthony Perri. Perri's education then took him to Jefferson Elementary School on Fillmore Street, where he attended from second grade to eighth grade, earning higher marks each year in school so that by the time he was finishing grade school, his marks were well into the eighties, equivalent to high B grades.

Perri prepared as best he could and moved to a high school with a great track record: Manley High School. Manley High School was east of Sacramento Boulevard and a few blocks north of Taylor Street. A few years prior to Anthony's attendance, in July 1933, Manley Junior High School had been reorganized into a senior high school with an elementary school inside the building. The two schools coexisted well for the next ten years. Anthony's grades signaled a smart student and an even harder worker. His grades continued to be A's and B's at the academically strong school.

ORIGINS: JOHN J. NAGLE

John J. Nagle Jr. was born to John and Ruth Nagle in 1936. The Nagle family established strong roots on Chicago's South Side. Specifically, John Nagle's family lived in Englewood, near Fifty-ninth and Bishop, when the neighborhood experienced dynamic growth. During the first half of the twentieth century, Englewood's population remained around ninety thousand residents. Aided by rail lines, Englewood's proximity to Chicago and public transportation were good ingredients in the neighborhood's recipe for growth. Englewood's stable economic presence led to large department stores with a strong Chicago presence, such as Sears. The Nagle family enjoyed the tranquil yet bustling life of Englewood with all of its amenities.

When it was time for John to attend high school, his parents desired to keep their strong Catholic roots and enrolled him at St. Rita High School, on the 6000 block of Claremont. St. Rita's was one of the religious high schools that served a strong Catholic community on Chicago's South Side. John's high school years stretched from 1951 to 1955. During high school, John set his gaze on a young lady two years younger than he was, Marlene. She lived across the street from him, just south of Garfield Boulevard, near the expressway. That proximity gave John ample opportunities to initiate a friendship that eventually led to romance.

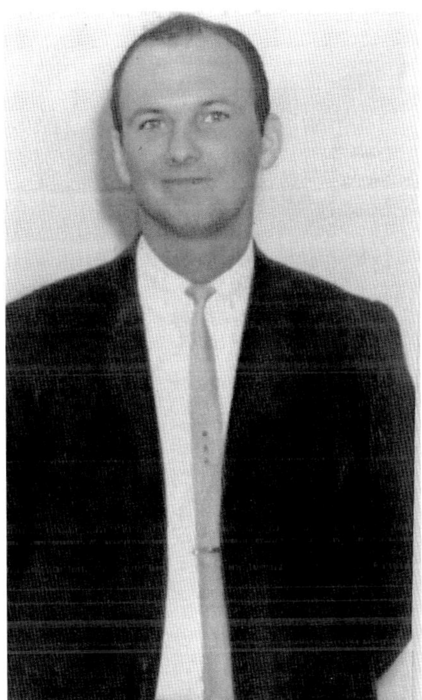

An official Northlake police photo of John Nagle. *Courtesy of Northlake Police Department.*

John and Marlene's romance eventually led to marriage. Their courtship included many days at Sherman Park, a park designed by well-known men such as Daniel Burnham and Frederick Law Olmsted. Sherman Park's purpose was to enrich the lives of the working-class immigrants in the surrounding areas. And for the Nagles, the park enriched their romantic lives. They were married young and started a family. John was only twenty-two years old when they had their firstborn son, John. The family eventually settled in Bellwood, another Chicago suburb that was close to John's work as a detective sergeant for the Northlake Police Department.

Nagle's strong Catholic upbringing influenced his activities. At St. Rita's, the Catholic Youth Organization hosted boxing tournaments. John became an avid boxer through the CYO. His strong hands, forearms and solid upper body provided him with a strong foundation to box. Nagle's active participation in high school and in church influenced him to become a police officer. He took his responsibilities as an officer seriously, practicing his shooting and eventually winning a shooting competition at the LaGrange Tournament.

By the fall of 1967, three parolees no longer reported to their assigned jobs. The certifications and training they received during their prison rehabilitation program were nullified. During those months, Henry Gargano and Clifton Daniels came across another former prisoner, Ronald Dale Raine. Together they discussed their former lives. Together they formed a crew and returned to their lives of crime. They returned to what they did best: stealing. That is what all three of them had done from their adolescent years. So the ingredients were mixed during the summer that culminated in the fall of 1967.

Chapter 2

OCTOBER 27, 1967

The Robbery

The Policemen

The morning of October 27, 1967, began not unlike any other morning for Northlake's residents. That morning's challenge included navigating through the four inches of snow covering the ground—surely an ominous sign. Inclement weather that early in the year served as an oddity. Northlake police officer Anthony Perri, a forty-one-year-old member of the police force, lived on a quaint residential street just under a mile from his job at the police station. He was married to Antoinette and was father to two teenagers. His pride and joy were his sixteen-year-old son, Ted, and twelve-year-old daughter, Ann Marie. In his eighth tour of duty, Perri worked a job he thoroughly enjoyed for a community he loved serving. Northlake served as the perfect town since he had moved his family there from Chicago's Little Italy.

His fellow policeman Detective Sergeant John J. Nagle was a thirty-one-year-old man, husband to Marlene and father to three sons. John, his eldest son, was nine years old. Following John were Robert, at seven years, and the youngest, Joseph, who was four years of age. Unbeknown to the Nagle family, two miles from their Bellwood, Illinois home were housed three men who would alter the lives of their families forever.

Antoinette Perri woke up that morning, prepared herself for work, woke up the kids and heard joyous sounds from her husband as he sang along to

Italian music. Perri was a happy-go-lucky man: "He loved to sing. He was a tenor, and he had a voice like Mario Lanza."[19] She enjoyed that about him. He was always upbeat, listened to music and sang along as best he could. Even on bad days, he brought a smile to her face that livened her up. "He had a marvelous sense of humor, always laughing and always happy."[20] She thought he was a typical Italian American.

The day before the Northlake Bank robbery, Antoinette accepted a job as a nurse's aide at the Villa Scalabrini Old People's Home, which was not far from their home.[21] She was excited about her work. She felt fulfilled as she helped others. She was a strong and maternal nurturer. Since the kids were a little older, she could be away from home during school hours. Besides, she was usually home for supper. The extra income helped their financial situation. Many Italian customs remained in their family.

The two had met decades earlier, in Chicago's Little Italy neighborhood. As a matter of fact, they met close to Taylor and Halsted Streets, the heart of Italian immigration. Growing up in the same neighborhood, they met and fell in love. Now they'd been married over twenty years, living the last sixteen years in suburban Northlake, one of the many suburbs Italians moved to as they progressed economically. Besides, things changed in Little Italy with Richard J. Daley's massive university project. Homes were torn down to build the University of Illinois at Chicago. A local Italian diaspora occurred.

Neither of them forgot their roots. Perri's strong immigrant work ethic was evident as he held down two jobs. "Perri, in addition to working about six hours a day as a Northlake policeman moonlighted as a laborer on the Chicago & North Western Railroad."[22] He enjoyed spending time with his kids and took them fishing whenever he had a chance. His eldest son, Ted, now sixteen years old, was big and broad shouldered and nearly as tall as he was. He played football on his high school team. His daughter, Ann Marie, was twelve years old and attended junior high school.

As Antoinette finished the last details of the morning, Anthony Perri and the kids looked out the window at the accumulated snow. Even by Chicago's standards, this much snow this early in the year was unusual. Antoinette took a quick look outside as she admired the beautiful white powder. The sun's rays reflected on a bright day. Perri made his way outside as he told them he needed to talk to the neighbors, clean the driveway and clean the entrance to the home. He shoveled the snow off the driveway and the concrete sidewalk to the front door. He walked over to the next-door neighbors, the Wolens, an older couple who had forged a friendship with the Perris. For the Perris, the Wolens embodied the city's reputation for friendly people.

Perri knocked on the Wolens' door. Victor Wolen answered, happy to see Anthony in his police uniform ready to leave for work. Perri asked Mr. Wolen for a favor. Mr. Wolen gladly obliged, as he knew they had a strong neighborly relationship. He then told Mr. Wolen that he expected a package later that day and that perhaps he might not be around to receive it. Mr. Wolen mentioned he would look out for the delivery and sign for it. Perri then reached into his pocket, pulled out some money and handed it over to Mr. Wolen. Perri smiled and realized he had good neighbors.

Perri walked back home, opened the door to his house and called for his family. As they walked to the car, Ann Marie's backpack bounced up and around as she eagerly headed for school. Ted joined his sister in the backseat as Antoinette sat in the front seat. Antoinette's face shined, as she was grateful for the great family she had. Besides, she felt safer in Northlake than in their old neighborhood. And with teenage children, that was probably a good thing—a very good thing.

However, as they drove to Villa Scalabrini to drop her off at work, she had a quick recall of the many previous conversations she and Anthony had had the past few months. She didn't have peace about the job her husband performed. It might only be six hours a day, but it was a dangerous job. Policemen were sometimes shot and killed. She wished he had a different job. "She hoped her husband would quit the force."[23] And for the last time ever, this united, ideal Italian American family gathered together as they rode along the snowy roads this late October morning.

Perri dropped his wife off at work, kissed her goodbye and then took the kids to school. He drove Ted to West Leyden High School, just down the road from Villa Scalabrini. Ann Marie was at Mannheim Junior High School, near the corner of Grand Avenue and Mannheim Road. Perri eagerly went to the Northlake Police Station, parked in the lot behind the building and entered through the back door as he started his day shift as a patrolman with the Northlake Police Department.

As for Detective Sergeant John Nagle of Bellwood, Illinois, being a police officer was his dream come true. To say he enjoyed being a police officer was to put it mildly. He lived for the job. So on the morning of October 27, 1967, he was so eager to start work that he awoke early, "not even waiting for the alarm clock to go off."[24] He was excited, just like every other day. His career and personal life were on the quick rise: three beautiful young kids, a faithful and lovely wife and a wonderful three-bedroom home close to his work.

Back in June, he had been named detective sergeant, a distinction he carried with honor and a sense of accomplishment. His wife, Marlene, later said, "He was very proud of that."[25] Besides, he was still very young, in his early thirties, and a bright future awaited him. That summer, he had taken the examination required for officers. He placed first among his peers.[26] Doing so well on the exam prompted his promotion to detective. Nagle was born to be a cop.

Like other residents of Chicago, the snow slightly altered his daily routine. After he awoke early in the morning, he prepared to go to work as he shoveled the snow around his home. His face shone with contentment. He happily served as a Northlake policeman.

He noticed that his older son, John, didn't have snow boots since he had outgrown them. John and Robert were both students at St. John Chrysostom, a Catholic school and parish recently founded a short distance away.[27] The drive was on the way to work: simply take Forty-ninth Avenue, the next street over, and head north a few short blocks to find the school and parish. The youngest, Joseph, stayed behind with his mom. He was only four years old, much too young for school. Nagle kissed his wife goodbye, telling his kids he would drive them to school this morning as a result of the snowfall. Marlene watched proudly as her husband and two kids left home. She never realized one of them would never return.

She reflected on her life with John, on her sons and on John's many attributes. Ever since Marlene had met John, she always described him as "vibrant, a man who was full of life."[28] And that is how Marlene remembered her husband.

However, John's work habit led to her concerns about the manner in which he responded to his work. That is, her husband usually arrived first on the scene, no matter what the emergency was. She often quipped to him, "Do you always have to be the first one on the scene?"[29] He often retorted immediately and added that he was now a detective sergeant—it was his duty to respond quickly. That kind of initiative made her nervous, though. As a matter of fact, that certain nervous feeling had never really left her since John had decided to join the force seven years ago.[30] There were dangerous people out there. She thought that was something policemen's wives lived with on a daily basis.

OCTOBER 27, 1967

THE ROBBERY

Clifton Orneal Daniels drove a gold-colored 1966 Buick Skylark headed for the Northlake Bank at 26 West North Avenue.[31] His two passengers were fellow criminals Henry Gargano, seated in the passenger seat, and Ronald Dale Raine, seated in the backseat. On the way to the bank, the three men discussed the last-minute details of their plan—be quick, efficient and effective. They were to stick to the plan, plain and simple, just as they had talked about it. And if any of them was caught, they needed to stick to their personal code of not divulging any information. They were to keep their mouths shut.

There was going to be a car parked along the bank's side street. The female driver of that car was going to cut off any traffic traveling through there. All they had to do after robbing the bank was follow her down the street. The escape would be easy for them. They would work together as a team. Then they would drop off the getaway vehicle as planned before returning back to their home base nearby. Although they had not done much surveillance

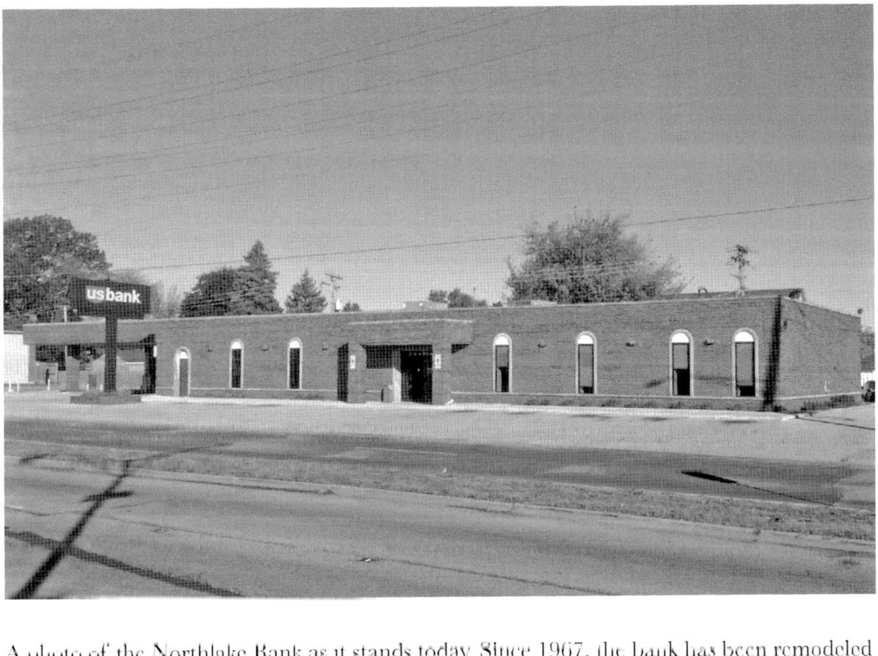

A photo of the Northlake Bank as it stands today. Since 1967, the bank has been remodeled and expanded, with the entrance now at center instead of bearing right. To the right of the bank lies the robbers' escape path. In 2017, Northlake will celebrate the fiftieth anniversary of the famous robbery. *Photo taken by Edgar Gamboa Návar.*

beforehand, the location of the bank was too good to be true. The bank had multiple escape routes, industrial corridors and a diverted police force.

Raine and Daniels had a bad feeling about this bank. They had decided to hit the bank only four days prior. Their usual strategy involved heavy reconnaissance with extensive strategy planning. In fact, Raine and the others liked that part of crime. Planning accordingly was part of the fun, Raine thought, but cash reserves were low for the group. They maintained a high lifestyle—a very high lifestyle, especially Gargano. Money left their hands just as quickly as they stole it. Raine spent about a month surveying Chicago-area banks but found "nothing suitable."[32] Raine and Daniels set aside their bad feelings about this robbery and decided to proceed with it, as Gargano suggested they do.

On the way to the bank, they took a circuitous route and stopped briefly to use a phone booth.[33] That phone booth was located outside the fenced-in area of Gate 2 at the south parking lot of Automatic Electric. Gargano stepped out of the vehicle, dialed the police phone number and diverted the majority of their force to a falsely overturned and incinerated gasoline truck on Wolf Road and Fullerton Avenue, on the other side of town from the police station.[34] There was gasoline all over the road, he told them. However, the policemen's search efforts proved fruitless—they didn't find an overturned truck. The squad car then proceeded north on Wolf Road to Grand Avenue before heading back south on Wolf Road to Geneva Street in search of the overturned gasoline truck. Nothing.

As the cops searched for the gasoline truck, Raine double-checked his nineteen-shell bandolier and assured himself he had enough shotgun shells for battle. Raine later said it was "Mexican *bandito* style."[35] He was armed with a twelve-gauge Winchester Model 1200 pump-action shotgun, the kind the military used in Vietnam. His fellow bandit Gargano had a .30-caliber U.S. Browning M1918 automatic rifle and a .38 Smith and Wesson Special, ironically the same gun used by many police departments to arm their forces. The weapons provided more than enough firepower—the thrill of adventure was just as important as the robbery. To the bandits, the cops were undermanned.

The Buick Skylark then proceeded to the bank and arrived at 10:41 a.m. It parked in front of the bank's entrance. As they stepped out of the car, Raine yelled, "Don't park here!"[36] Although there was nothing unusual at the Northlake Bank, a police car sped away moments before they arrived. For Raine, it was a premonition.

Several cars were parked outside, including a van with the words "Northlake Heating Company" written across it. That van belonged to a worker in the basement who was preparing the bank's heating equipment for winter. The early snowfall gave residents reasons to prepare for winter early that year. People conversed about the snowfall that morning. A typical October in a Chicago suburb.

Daniels stepped out of the car armed with a .45-caliber Colt automatic pistol. His disguise was befitting of Halloween in a few days: it included a blue shirt under a gray cloth zippered jacket, dark blue pants, black shoes, a dark cloth hat, a blue bandanna and sunglasses. Raine followed him sporting a ski mask, sunglasses and a dark-colored, full-length raincoat with his bandolier around his left shoulder, his pump-action shotgun and .38 revolver tucked on the inside waistband of his dark pants. Gargano's dress comprised a blue bandanna, a gray jacket, dark pants and a hat.[37] The time to act on the crime had come. This robbery was just another one in the long list of crimes they had performed in the past several months.

For the most part, Northlake Bank was a typical suburban bank focused on customer service and daily transactions from a strong and developing middle class. Small- to medium-sized loans were common, as Northlake had many first-time home buyers. A typical workforce consisted of approximately fifteen employees, including tellers and bankers, and an executive present on the premises. The bank had six tellers' cages, many of them busy during business hours. The bank's double doors gave a clear view from inside the bank to people entering and a clear view of the lobby to those approaching the bank. The bank's open view of doors and windows was something that bandits desired.

As a result of growth in the area, the need for a local bank had emerged, and Northlake Bank secured its stake to the expanding riches of the baby-boomer generation. The suburb's strategic location provided quick access to companies in the O'Hare Airport area.

The Northlake Bank had been under surveillance for several weeks as the Northlake Police Department had received warnings that it was to be robbed. Northlake police took precautionary steps in securing the area. Squad cars were parked near several area businesses, not just the bank. As time passed, those fears subsided, and the extra attention was no longer warranted as no threat seemed legitimate.

That particular Friday was unusually busy, as most Fridays tended to be since the nearby industrial firms cashed checks that day. That was one of the blessings of this bank in this industrial suburb and also one of its curses. That meant more money on the premises at the end of the work week. Any bank robbery should fetch well into tens of thousands of dollars. Bank executives accordingly planted decoy money in tellers' cages and in the vault. As a precautionary move, every bank employee knew that any robbery attempt required them to give the decoy money. That was the bank's policy—unmarked currency to the naked eye. It was a cat and mouse game. Any would-be thief required proper preparation if he was to rob the Northlake Bank.

Suddenly three gunmen charged the bank as they waved and shouted, "Everyone down on the floor! Get down! Get down!"[38] Gargano and the others scolded them, "If you ring an alarm, we won't hesitate to kill you. Get down on the floor or we'll shoot you. Get down on the floor or else you'll be killed."[39] "Don't ring the buzzers. We will kill everybody."[40]

Sitting at his desk, Vice-President Richard Hank noticed the burst into the bank, quickly detecting the masked perpetrators. A bank teller used her foot to even more quickly press the silent alarm button that rang three blocks east of the bank to the momentarily depleted Northlake Police Department.[41] Along with the fifteen employees working that morning were seven customers who willingly obeyed the direct orders of Gargano and lay down on the cold floor as they stared down the barrel of his high-powered weapon.[42] Of those fifteen employees, five worked in the tellers' cages, four women and a man. The peaceful Friday morning scene a few moments earlier suddenly became tense.

Without hesitation, Daniels and Raine ran and jumped over the end counter behind the five tellers' cages. Daniels quickly emptied two female tellers' counters of cash and shoved the bills into his black zippered bag as Raine jolted toward the vault with his white pillowcase and readily placed cash in it.[43] As the two thieves clenched dollar bills, Gargano briefly left the hostages unattended, climbed over the counter and put handfuls of money into his black plastic bag from the other tellers' counters.[44] He pulled out a pry bar and tried to open teller register No. 2. His unsuccessful attempt frustrated him, and he dropped the pry bar. The bar landed near the bank employee hostage crouching on the floor just underneath her teller's cage. He then realized they needed to leave soon. The hostages remained facedown during this brief ordeal as they wondered what might be next. They feared never walking out of the bank alive.

The bandits' goal was to go in and out of the bank in no more than a minute. In and out before anyone realized what had transpired, just like they planned. They wound up staying there about two minutes and fifteen seconds. There was simply too much money to be taken.

Daniels retrieved more money from behind the counter as Raine and Gargano quickly marched toward the front door. Raine told his fellow thieves, "We've got a lot of money."[45] Then he replaced his mask with sunglasses and yelled to Daniels, "Come on! Come on!"[46] "Watch out for cops!" Raine remarked as they left the bank.[47] Raine walked through the bank's doors. As Daniels climbed back over the counter ready to follow his comrades, he heard shooting just beyond the first glass set of double doors they had entered less than two and a half minutes earlier.

The bandits' well-conceived strategy did not allow them to foresee the police car that pulled into the parking lot as they exited. They intended to make their way to the getaway car that was parked right outside the bank. The alarm that had been tripped a few minutes prior was answered by two policemen, Michael Cain and Anthony Perri, in Northlake Police Department's marked squad car No. 602. Sergeant John Nagle and Officer Ernest Hustedt quickly followed them in a second unmarked squad car. All four of them arrived at the bank in less than two minutes.[48]

When the initial alarm rang in the police department, it was taken seriously but with some reservation, as false alarms were reported regularly at the bank. As Cain and Perri walked out of the police station, Cain quickly commented about grabbing an additional shotgun. Perri retorted by saying there was no need, as they would likely return to the station in a short amount of time.[49] They made their way out of the parking lot and hurried to the bank a few blocks away. They parked their marked squad car at an angle just outside the bank's doors, behind a 1966 Buick Skylark. The cops had no idea who had driven that Buick Skylark minutes beforehand.

Officer Cain initially noticed a rifle poking out of the door and quickly thereafter heard and saw bullets fly in his direction. Gargano and Raine spotted the police cruiser out of the corner of their eyes as they approached the outer glass double doors. They initiated a firefight before the police car came to a stop. The bullets flew at the officers. Cain yelled at Perri, "Get down! Get down!" as he grabbed Perri by the head and forced him down in his seat as a bullet pierced through his passenger's side window, whizzing by them and then through the driver's side window.[50]

A barrage of bullets came straight at them and ricocheted off the engine block and metal ridges. Those metal ridges served as a barrier that ultimately saved Cain's life.[51] One bullet, however, hit Perri—he was struck in the head as he attempted to crawl out of the vehicle with his shotgun and valiantly attempted to return fire. Raine noticed the officer crawling out of the vehicle, ran up to him and shot him in the head at close range. That dealt him a fatal blow.[52] Perri's body lay on the ground, bleeding and clinging to life with every last heartbeat this side of eternity. He continued to twitch. Cain was grazed in the right arm as he crouched down in the footwall of the car and was temporarily unable to return fire.[53] Everything happened so fast for the officers. They were simply caught off guard.

The bandits' military-style automatic weapons proved to be too overwhelming for the cops and their handguns as a flurry of bullets continued to fly at them like a torrential rainstorm.

Gargano noticed that Officer Cain was still in the vehicle and yelled, "There is one of them who's in the squad car. I'll get him, too" as he took a shot that went through the car, missing its intended target.[54]

Just then, the second squad car entered the parking lot ready to engage in the gunfight. Officers Nagle and Hustedt jolted out of the vehicle. Nagle stood beside his squad car holding his shotgun in plain view of the culprits and, as it turned out, in plain view of the bullets. In a brief moment, Cain popped out of his crouch, a stream of blood running down his face, aimed his gun at Raine and struck him. Raine went down near the sidewalk with a wound to the neck, dropping his Winchester shotgun as he yelled, "I'm hit!"[55] The bullet penetrated Raine's neck, bouncing off his vertebrae and coming out through the top portion of his shoulder. Facing up, Raine's body lay motionless.

In the meantime, Daniels ran through the bank doors to the parked 1966 Buick Skylark ready to make his getaway with the others as another cop received a fatal hit as well. As Daniels ran to the car, Gargano shot Officer Nagle, striking him in the head with a bullet that hit his left upper cheek and ended his life.[56] Nagle was also hit in the abdomen as blood spattered onto his car. His body fell to the ground and lay facedown. Three total bullets went through the windshield of his unmarked squad car. A gunshot blast's debris wounded his partner, Hustedt, as he held his face in agony and screamed.[57]

Gargano seized the opportunity of a wounded police officer lying on the pavement. He stood near Perri as he leaned over the hood of the car and shot additional bullets from his pistol into the patrolman's body, realizing life had not yet left him.[58] Officer Perri sustained twelve total body shots in a handful of seconds.[59] That served as a testament to the bandits' hatred of law enforcement.

The air in the area reverberated with the sound of flying bullets. Two additional law enforcement agents entered the battle. An alarm sounded on police car radios that tipped off officers in the nearby vicinity about the fierce clash.[60]

Another officer became a willing and crucial participant as he drove by the scene on his way to work as a policeman in Schaumburg. William Bartkavich dropped off some dirty uniforms at the Martinizing Cleaners, almost in front of the police station, two blocks east of Wolf Road. He saw white smoke and heard the fiery gunshot exchange a few blocks away. Instantly, he jumped into his car and drove as close to the scene as possible. The traffic jam slightly deterred him as people watched the morning's events unfold.[61] Due to the traffic, Bartkavich parked his car near the Jewel supermarket and ran toward the bank. Bartkavich stopped as he barricaded himself in between the parked cars. His heart raced, and he joined the gun battle as he ran with his revolver in hand.[62] He was mesmerized as he saw "a tall man with an automatic weapon lean over the hood of a car and shoot Perri."[63] He assisted his hometown officers, shooting once, hitting Gargano and dealing him a severe wound in his upper right arm that forced Gargano to drop his assault rifle and a bag of money as he clutched his bleeding limb.[64] Gargano "staggered, and winced in pain."[65] Gargano noticed Daniels in the getaway car and feared that he might also be left behind, so he yelled to Daniels as he grabbed the car's hood ornament and held himself up.[66] Daniels backed into the marked police car, which was parked directly behind. Raine's last-minute suggestion of not parking there proved wise. They bumped other cars as they exited the parking lot.

In the midst of the fierce Vietnam-style war zone, Daniels drove the Buick a few feet to where Gargano stood in pain. Daniels exited the vehicle to help Gargano but then realized Raine lay on the pavement because of the shot he'd received. He picked up a bag of cash underneath a car and Raine's shotgun as he noticed Gargano's blood smeared on the side of the Buick Skylark. He quickly decided to retrace a few steps back to the car and drove it closer to Gargano, opened the door for him and shouted to him, "Get in! Get in!"[67] Gargano then shuffled his feet to the passenger's side and climbed in as he left both a trail of blood behind him and his bag of money, which he had taken just a few minutes prior.

As the car sped away, they bumped another car out of the way. Another officer heard the shooting at a nearby shopping center and rushed to witness the massacre firsthand. Sergeant Orrin Deckert arrived at the scene and got a shotgun blast off at the fleeing vehicle.[68] Bartkavich eventually fired his .38-caliber .357 Colt Magnum three more times and assured himself he'd made a direct hit on one of them because "he saw blood spurt from the man's shoulder."[69]

Escape Routes

Thwarting police after a bank robbery is imperative as a good escape route is essential. And although the robbers' plan did not anticipate the intense firefight minutes before they fled, Northlake's burgeoning roads catered to such an escape. To best understand Northlake's prime location with multiple exit strategies as it relates to the robbers, we need to grasp the area's development.

The suburbs of western Cook County experienced great growth during the 1960s as their proximity to one of the nation's busiest airports proved fertile ground for large corporations that needed to meet their logistical demands. Northlake wasn't any different. Burny Brothers Bakery, Scholle Chemical Corporation and Dominick's were a few companies that took advantage of the town's strategic location. A person who drove through the major thoroughfare associated the town more with the bakery aroma of bread, cake and cookies that permeated the air than with anything else. Mom-and-pop shops lined the central business district along North Avenue.

To accommodate workers at the Buick Defense plant in nearby Melrose Park and at other local factories, Midland Corporation developed a large plot of land around North Avenue and Wolf Road. They built many "shell houses" that needed carpentry, electrical work and plumbing. Bedrooms were built on the second floor. Owners invested their energies in building homes out of these shell houses.

Few well-established communities existed in the 1930s and 1940s west of Harlem Avenue in Chicago. By the 1960s, the landscape was different. Midland Corporation invested in land alongside North Avenue, hoping people would rather live close to work. The former site of the Westward Ho Golf Club provided enough land for hundreds of houses, a park and a home for the aged. Midland decided to take the risk.

In a matter of two years, nearly six hundred "shell homes" were built, thus creating a village. Northlake incorporated into a city in 1949. People from

Chicago moved west, and Northlake was one of their towns of choice. By the 1960s, Northlake had experienced tremendous growth. Supermarkets, such as Jewel, and other large businesses were established. A shopping center was built in the center of town to accommodate Northlake's growth. Residents such as the Perris liked the growing town's amenities, including solid schools for their children.

THE NORTHLAKE BANK was built alongside North Avenue, a critical artery that led through the heart of these west Cook County industrial suburbs. To the west was the Tri-State Tollway, less than a mile from the bank. To the east, Mannheim Road provided north–south access. Lake Street cut diagonally through the south portion of town connecting North Avenue to Mannheim Road, a great street for a getaway. Many of these access points were built in the previous decade of the 1950s, which made the Northlake Bank a great choice for a bank robbery—and in the minds of the bandits, an easy choice, with or without much planning.

DANIELS DROVE THE CAR on Lavergne Avenue, the street that bordered the bank. Lavergne Avenue was a two-way street that led to a development that sat on a former golf course. As planned, a white Ford with a female driver blocked the intersection of Lavergne and Westward Ho Drive so that no traffic passed through there except the bandits. The woman who drove that car quickly lowered her foot down on the gas pedal and led the way for the robbers.

The Buick Skylark darted north on Lavergne Avenue for half a block before it turned west on Westward Ho Drive, the street behind the Northlake Bank. Daniels reached over to pull a slumped Gargano toward him. The masked Gargano rode in the passenger's side as he clutched his arm, slightly leaning forward and grimacing in pain. The Buick Skylark accelerated and continued past Hillside Avenue, where Daniels tossed out a brass cartridge case as he attempted to reload his weapon. On the following street, Harvard Avenue, they turned south toward North Avenue. Daniels steered the Skylark on the service road toward the Scholle Chemical Coporation parking lot. As they drove, Daniels asked Gargano if the bleeding had stopped. Gargano, in pain, mentioned that he thought Raine accidentally shot him in the confusion of the gunfight.[70] Everything happened so fast. The other times they had escaped easily—not this time, though.

With multiple escape exits that included Intrastate 294, the bandits' vital escape plan included switching cars—from the 1966 Buick Skylark to a 1966

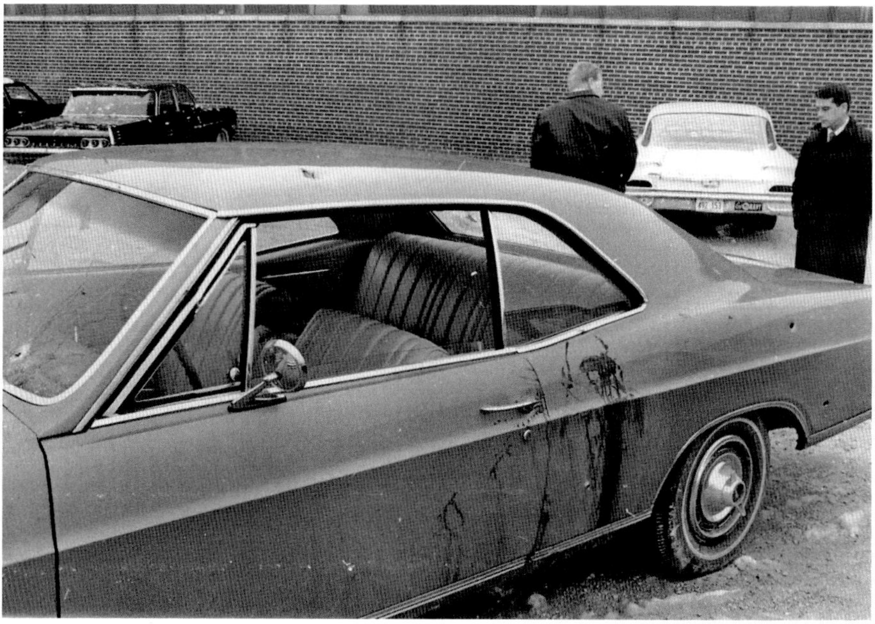

The getaway car driven by Clifton Daniels and Henry Gargano from the Northlake Bank to Scholle Chemical Corporation—notice Gargano's blood smeared on the vehicle. *Courtesy of the Northlake Police Department.*

four-door Chevrolet Bel-Air parked in the Scholle Chemical Coporation plant parking lot, about two miles west of the Northlake Bank.[71] Daniels slammed the brakes, and the car came to a screeching halt. He quickly transferred the black bag full of cash and weapons and his fellow criminal to the gray vehicle stationed among the others with the help of their female accomplice. Daniels knew his window to escape was quickly evaporating. He wasn't sure, but he later thought he'd left another bag of money in the car.

The bandits drove north away from North Avenue and toward Fullerton Avenue and then east on Fullerton Avenue. They turned north on Mannheim Road and immersed themselves into regular traffic. Gargano, however, bled profusely as their female accomplice tended to him in the backseat.

As the adrenaline pumped through their bodies from the bank robbery, Daniels drove aggressively, deciding that Mannheim Road provided the best access point before they headed to their home base of operations. Gargano bled profusely as he wondered what to do next. The woman grabbed a rag and handed it to Gargano so he could put some pressure on the wound and stop the bleeding. The bleeding continued, staining his jacket and dripping onto the seat. Gargano also used an overcoat to apply whatever pressure he could to the wound.

They headed north on Mannheim Road with the intent of taking Irving Park Road. Before they reached Grand Avenue in suburban Franklin Park, Daniels remembered seeing a medical clinic, the Leyden Medical Center. They hoped for discretionary assistance. He pulled into the parking lot, stepped out of the car, headed to the clinic's main door and pounded on it furiously as he looked for help.[72] Gargano lay in the backseat with their female accomplice, in agony from the gun wound. The clinic was closed. A custodial worker slightly opened the door and told him that the clinic didn't open until noon. It was 11:20 a.m. Daniels rushed back into the vehicle and sped north on Mannheim, sweating as much as Gargano bled.

They continued north on Mannheim to Irving Park Road, where they tossed one of the masks they'd used during the robbery out of the window. They needed to get rid of every bit of evidence. Daniels drove the Chevy Bel-Air home to 610 Twenty-fourth Street in Bellwood, Illinois.[73] They parked the car in the nearly leaning garage that backed up to an alley.

Daniels grabbed Gargano, putting his arm around his waist as Gargano wrapped his left arm around Daniels's neck, and helped him up the two flights of stairs to the second-floor apartment and to a temporary safe haven.[74] The apartment's main resident had been left behind. The apartment was technically rented by Ronald Dale Raine. He, now in police custody, lay wounded and was likely headed to a hospital. Their run of successful robberies finally faced obstacles, but Raine had his own problems.

Unbeknownst to Gargano and Daniels, another home near their Bellwood apartment received much attention. Ironically, their apartment was less than two miles from one of their victims, Detective Sergeant John Nagle. Reporters and investigators spent many hours in John Nagle's home in the next few days as they interviewed his widow and learned more about Detective Nagle. Daniels and Gargano connected the dots quickly as they read newspapers and heard reports of Detective John Nagle. Staying that close to their victim's home was simply too risky.

Daniels led Gargano to one of two bedrooms in the second-floor apartment. Gargano lay down on the mattress as he cursed up a storm and yelled at the throbbing pain he felt in his immovable arm. Gargano's blood freely flowed from his arm to the bed. The huge stains penetrated the mattress. Gargano yelled at Daniels to get something for his arm. Daniels reacted instantly as he ran to the bathroom and grabbed some rags and towels to stop the bleeding.

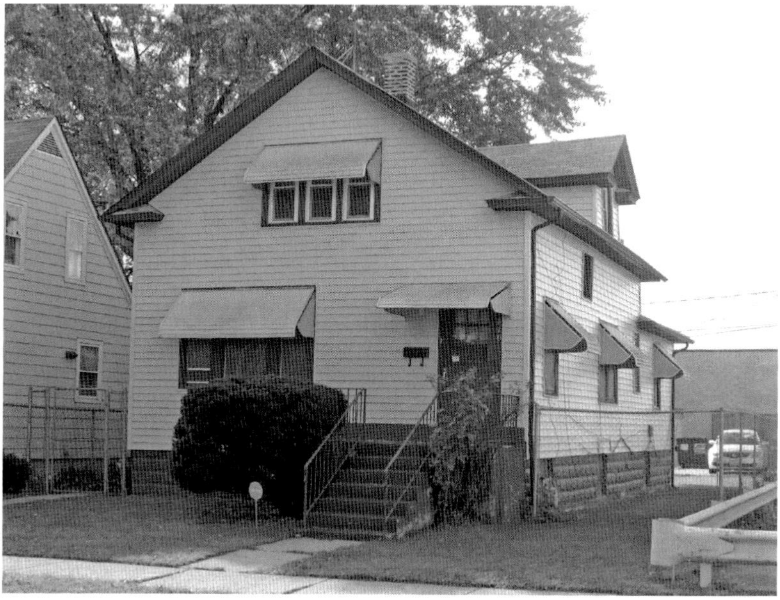

A modern-day image of the house where the Northlake Bank robbers lived for several months and briefly took refuge after their bank robbery. *Photo taken by Edgar Gamboa Návar.*

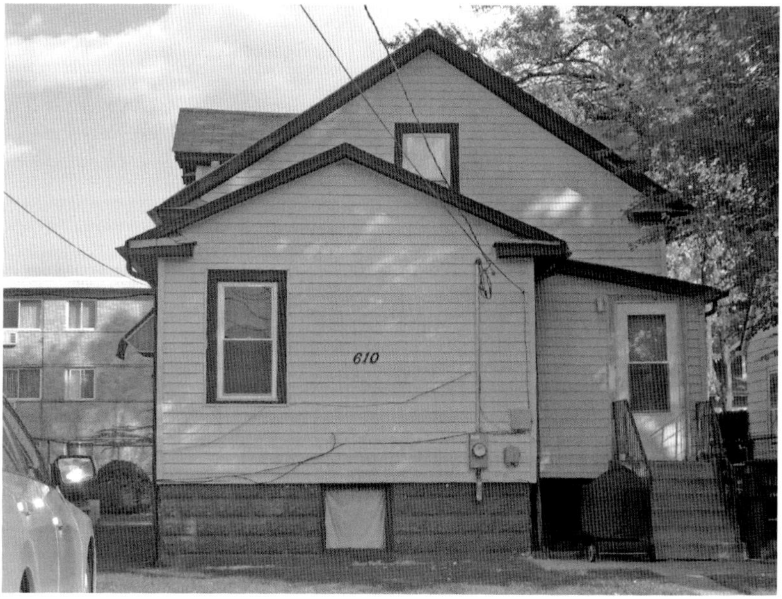

The rear entrance to the Northlake Bank robbers' second-floor apartment. Daniels carried Gargano up these stairs as he bled from a gunshot wound. *Photo taken by Edgar Gamboa Návar.*

Daniels covered the arm with the rags, but nothing stopped the bleeding. He couldn't apply too much pressure to the wound since Gargano felt so much pain.

Daniels and their female accomplice felt the adrenaline that ran through their bodies. Gargano yelled out commands as the bleeding continued. If the cops showed up here, they were headed back to jail. Gargano was done with prison life. He and Daniels would go down shooting. As he liked to say, "Shoot to kill." Ironically, his statement rang true that day. He shot to kill, and he was shot in return. Their female accomplice thought twice about all that.

Daniels ran back and forth in the apartment. He thought there were some bandages in the bathroom that their female accomplice could wrap around Gargano's arm. Quickly, Daniels ran to the bathroom and grabbed them, hoping the bleeding would stop. The female accomplice slowly wrapped Gargano's arm. Gargano felt this was a losing battle. There was simply too much bleeding. There weren't enough rags, towels or bandages to stop it. She mentioned calling his sister, Annette, for help. She was finished. Daniels suggested that calling Annette was a good idea. Maybe Annette could deal with the bleeding better than both of them. Their female accomplice departed as Daniels's adrenaline slightly subsided.

Aside from Gargano's bleeding, the afternoon was low key for the fugitives—nothing compared to the excitement of that morning. Daniels thought about how this well-planned excursion had not gone as well as the other ones. He quickly picked up the phone and dialed it. On the other end, Annette Leonardo, the sister of the wounded Gargano, picked up. Daniels explained that her brother had been shot in the upper right arm near the shoulder. He explained the wound's severity. Annette, not surprised at all by Daniels's comments, decided to drive over quickly to the apartment to help her brother, making the nearly hour-long drive from Bolingbrook to Bellwood. The first thing she did, though, was rent a car—anything that wouldn't lead back to her so easily.

Later that afternoon, Annette arrived. She looked at the wound and wondered how her brother was still alive. He couldn't move his arm. She thought the arm was likely broken. Like a good sister, she tended to the wound throughout that afternoon and into the evening, knowing she couldn't leave the apartment.

Daniels turned to the radio, now eager to find out if the robbery had made the news. He quickly searched for a station with the latest news. All three persons heard that two policemen were killed in a Northlake Bank robbery just outside Chicago. There was no shortage of news. They listened to the news report on the Grundig KS750U console Raine had purchased sometime prior in Old Town at Oakley Furniture Store, about a mile from Gargano's girlfriend's apartment, their next stop as fugitives.

A Macabre Scene

Michael Tenore, one of the officers sent to the falsely reported overturned gasoline truck a mile away, heard about the robbery at the Northlake Bank over the police radio. The police radio became extremely active with yells of "Help us! We're being shot! Bank alarm!"[75] He noticed the bodies of policemen lying on the pavement after he arrived at the macabre scene. There were "shattered bodies and shattered machines."[76] "It was a scene to match some very tough scenes in the annals of American hold-up violence."[77] The carnage created by the military weapons was simply too much for the police officers to handle. To say the officers were outgunned would be an understatement as they only got a few shots off, most of them from those who responded to the ongoing bank robbery they'd heard about over the police radio, and mostly after the perpetrators left the scene.

Fellow Officer Hustedt continually lifted his hand to his face as he yelled from the gunshot blast while he still gripped his revolver. Detective Nagle lay facedown in a pool of his own blood near the front wheel of a blue Chevrolet. His gun lay on the ground just inches from his right hand. His left arm was crumpled underneath his body's weight. The other officer, Anthony Perri, sat with his back near the left front wheel of his squad car. The back of his head was blown out—he was dead.

Without hesitation, additional officers and ambulances arrived, shocked by what they saw. The two officers' vitals proved that they were dead. One of the bandits lay on the pavement but was still alive. Next to him were his bandolier, two Smith and Wesson guns and an automatic rifle that had caused the majority of the damage.

The wounded bandit, Raine, and the officers were taken to Northlake Community Hospital, a little more than a mile from the Northlake Bank. Officer Ernest Hustedt yelled in response to the gun blast to the face and was taken to the next town's hospital, Elmhurst Community Hospital. He feared

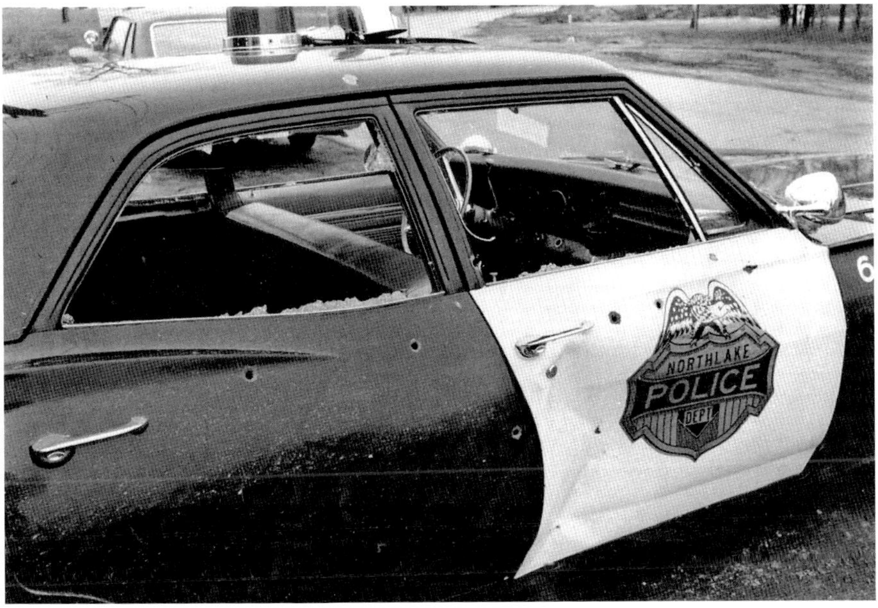

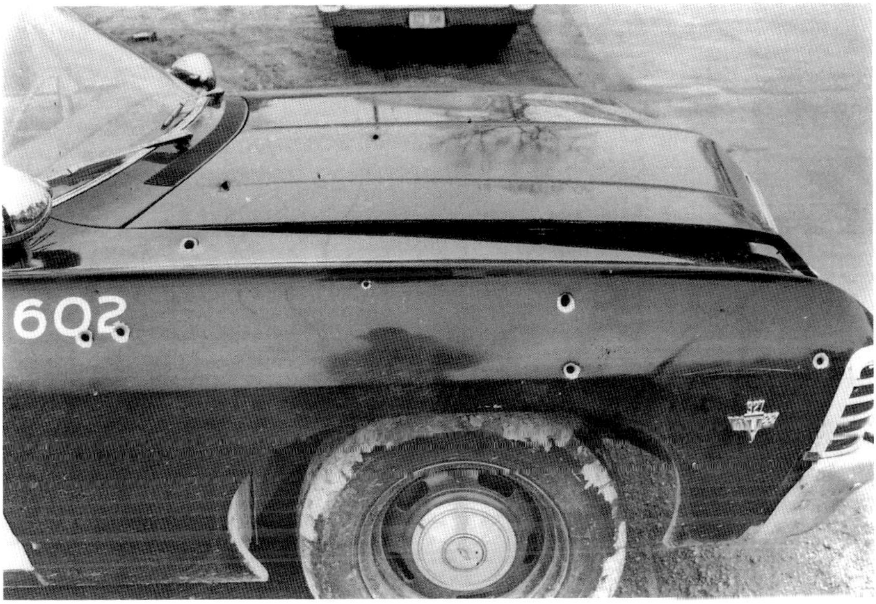

The squad car driven by Michael Cain and Anthony Perri to the Northlake Bank. The car received a smattering of bullets. *Courtesy of the Northlake Police Department.*

he might lose his sight as he screamed, "I can't see! I can't see!"[78] Officer Hustedt eventually recovered from the gunshot blast and survived.

Ironically, Raine and Officer Perri lay on gurneys in emergency rooms next to each other, only minutes after they crossed each other's paths—one sought to rob a bank, the other sought to stop him. Perri and Nagle were officially declared dead at 11:15 a.m. Both men died serving the Northlake community. Perri's own son identified him later that afternoon. Nagle's uncle, Robert, identified him.

The Investigation

Northlake police chief James Dean Gilliam speedily began the investigation as it pertained to the persons involved. He pieced the puzzle together—the phone calls, the warning signs and the style of robbery. To lose one officer was difficult, but to lose two officers was disheartening. Officer Perri's squad car No. 602 sustained over twenty shots of the more than one hundred bullets fired during the gun battle as its windows were shot out.[79] He was shocked by the amount of violence. Gilliam had never seen a scene that compared to this one over the course of his career.

Gilliam realized his two dead officers were Anthony Perri and John Nagle, two multi-year veterans of the police force. They both had young children. They were to notify those kids of their fatherless future. They were hardworking, dedicated police officers. Just as important, though, was that they prevented the gang from attacking again and having another shootout. Acting quickly was a necessity, not an option.

The Federal Bureau of Investigation that was set up during another era of bank robberies became immediately involved. The FBI was founded in the 1910s on investigating "violations of laws involving national banking."[80] Federal crimes were initially sparse. As the FBI's role increased during the next several decades, the bureau's techniques in solving cases required developing new techniques. Ironically, during the early years of Director J. Edgar Hoover, the FBI established an Identification Division. By the early 1920s, many large cities had initiated their own fingerprinting collections.[81] That became a useful tool to track down criminals. Matching crime scene fingerprints with established databases proved fruitful in apprehending criminals.

The head of the FBI Chicago office, Marlin W. Johnson quickly issued an alert in attempting to find the suspects. The FBI focused on the evidence and pieced the bandits' lives together. They focused on tracing the bandits' activities and possible hideouts. The FBI was also responsible for interviewing Marion inmates to determine if the crime gang worked as a network of former criminals. Their task also included examining fingerprints to apprehend the assailants. The bank, the escaped vehicle and weapons were to be dusted for fingerprints. The empty shell casings needed to be taken as evidence with the purpose of linking them to other crimes. Many saw the FBI as doing a lot of paperwork. The FBI saw itself as piecing together puzzles. The bank robbery and murders were now federal crimes.

Local police responsibilities included canvassing the area in hopes of finding the perpetrators hiding somewhere in the vicinity. They thought the assailants likely had local accomplices. To catch the thieves required groundwork, and the FBI provided that groundwork. Police set up perimeters; door-to-door engagement was essential, which kept the bandits uneasy. That was part of the FBI's strategy. As the FBI and local law enforcement worked together, there was an exponentially higher chance of catching the robbers. In law enforcement's minds, the multi-pronged effort usually proved successful.

Their cohesive approach started with one clue: the blood-smeared car was clear of any snow although several inches of snow had fallen that morning. They needed to look for a garage where the car had been kept overnight. The only marks on the car was one of the shooting victims' blood. A dwelling with a garage was the starting point.

Chief Gilliam maintained a quiet confidence as he met with Raine at the Northlake Community Hospital. Raine was strong enough to talk. Chief Gilliam and FBI agents interrogated him. They informed him of his rights. Raine was soon charged with two counts of murder and federal bank robbery. A warrant for his arrest was issued.[82] He initially refused to disclose any other information. Their gang had a personal code they adhered to among themselves. Ratting one another out was strictly forbidden. However, he mumbled, "I must have been hit early because I don't remember much about it."[83] That statement rang true and demonstrated his defiance.

During their conversation, Raine further revealed his actions two nights prior to the robbery. On October 25, 1967, he and two other persons, a husband-and-wife team, traveled to St. Louis and then spent Thursday night in a motel near Kankakee, about one and a half hours from his rented apartment in Bellwood.[84] Nothing out of the ordinary. Raine contemplated turning his life around—he wanted to change. He wanted to leave his life of crime behind. Things were difficult though. Gargano and Daniels persisted in continuing their criminal behavior. Raine's criminal records were primarily in the state of Washington, not in Illinois. Now he was participating in more dangerous crimes in Illinois. The traveling group eventually arrived back in the Chicago area on October 26. That was the day before the robbery. Raine connected with Gargano and Daniels to carry out their briefly preplanned bank robbery, but first, they needed an undetected getaway car.

THE GANG AWOKE early on Friday morning at 2:30 a.m. and drove slightly out of their route to a college campus near Lockport. They were determined to commit more robberies. And successful robberies would require undetected cars. Auto theft, a specialty of Ronald Dale Raine, was critical to their mission. As they arrived on campus, they scouted around for easy prey.

Lewis College, a Catholic school founded on the values of Jean-Baptiste de La Salle and on the teachings of St. John the Baptist, was on the verge of having one fewer vehicle on its campus that morning. The three coordinated to steal a Buick Skylark they detected as useful for the events later that day. The Buick Skylark was parked among other student vehicles in the Founders Hall parking lot. Quickly operating as a team, they managed to break into the car with a coat hanger, start it with a GM master key and drive away. A simple and quick task was completed—Raine's specialty. Later that day, the student's Buick Skylark made news around the Midwest with bullet holes in its windshield and bloodstains from a fugitive. Gargano and the others decided to head back to Chicago. There was another mission to complete before day's end. The goal was to be in possession of tens of thousands of dollars before the day was over. That was more than enough money to live the lifestyle they loved to live. Gargano thought of the many privileges of being out of prison. They had girls, they had drugs and soon they would have a lot more money.

LAW ENFORCEMENT TRANSFERRED Raine from Northlake Community Hospital to Bridewell Prison Hospital in Chicago, at Twenty-sixth Street and California Avenue. Bridewell was for short-term prisoners, typically those who waited for the outcomes of their trials at the House of Corrections. The county jail, however, operated as a separate entity. By the 1950s, short-term prisoners were being sentenced to more than five years.[85] Two years after the Northlake Bank robbery, the Illinois state legislature combined the county jail and the house of corrections under a single authority.

Raine remained heavily guarded. The doctor reported he was in fair condition, though he wasn't talking much. And the little that he said was intended to keep the authorities from accomplishing their mission: to capture his fellow gang members.

THE INVESTIGATION TEAM speedily asked witnesses for their account of the bank robbery. Several of the Northlake Bank's windows had bullet holes from the ferocious gunfight. That included many of the patrons' vehicles, important evidence in the bandits' future trials. Shell casings littered the bank's parking lot.

Inside that bank were seven customers, one of them a three-year-old boy named Mike Masella, who was waiting with his mother when the gunmen stormed in. His mom, Stella Masella, was trying to arrange a personal loan, one of the many loan applications the bank was handling during that time. As the men entered the building, Stella jumped on top of Mike, willing to sacrifice her life for his. All she thought about was saving her son's life. One of the bullets grazed her, and blood slowly trickled down onto her son.[86] The sound of gunfire was overwhelming, startling young Mike.

Another witness, assistant vice-president of the bank Gordon Ramsey, said, "There was little conversation during the holdup."[87] As the robbers left the building, they "opened up with automatic weapons fire through the outer set of glass doors while still in the building."[88] Ramsey later said that he "tried to see as little as possible."[89] Ramsey felt a rush of adrenaline as he laid on the marble floor and covered his head as he interlocked his fingers. He hoped the robbery soon passed.

THE POLICE INTERROGATED Raine—not much came out of him. He gave a false name. That placed a higher value on his companions than on justice. Then again, the police quickly realized that he and justice had been on opposite ends his entire life. As he received medical treatment, Raine, not completely in power of his own faculties, mentioned two names: James and Deborah Louise Stewart. He also mumbled "Randall" and "Jimmy." The police wanted more, but that was a start and a place to search. They knew the Stewarts of Melrose Park, another growing industrial suburb. They raced to their home.

The cops assured themselves of who they had in custody after they took the culprit's fingerprints. The mumbled names didn't suffice. The police needed hard evidence. And this was the perfect time to gather that information. The authorities found out something that only enraged them more and created a greater sense of urgency—an urgency that gave precedence to this case on a federal level. The man on this gurney was Ronald Dale Raine, originally from Yakima, Washington, and most recently from St. Louis, Missouri—a convicted criminal. Initial reports soon surfaced. He had a record of a life of crime.

Raine had a criminal record longer than most crooks:

1950: Robbery and burglary[90]
1954: Armed robbery
1955: Assault, first degree
1962: Interstate transportation of firearm after conviction

Raine was no Boy Scout. He was experienced, he had a history of theft, and most importantly, he liked guns—especially powerful guns. Using high-powered machine guns seemed to be his taste.

Getting the News

During the morning hours of October 27, 1967, Marlene Nagle focused on the day's tasks as she cleaned the home for the weekend and prepared the meal for later that day. Joseph was intent on enjoying the news of the day thus far as he looked out the window at the snow-covered grounds amid the Halloween decorations in the neighbor's home. Perhaps when his siblings arrived from school, he thought, they could go outside and play for a while. In the meantime, his toys needed his attention.

Marlene turned on the radio and listened to music and news as the day's events unfolded. A news update immediately sounded the alarm in her head and heart. A bank robbery had occurred moments earlier in the Chicago suburb of Northlake. Shooting was heard in the surrounding area. She froze, thinking, "Could John be involved?" She quickly dismissed that thought. After all, he was a detective sergeant who arrived first on the scene but also avoided deadly confrontation.

She remembered the time not too long ago when he had apprehended a robber armed with three guns without a shot being fired.[91] He was trained for this. The shooting, however, is what began to make her nervous. As the news report reverted back to its programming, she sat down on a chair, her knee slightly twitching because of nervousness, and simply "waited and hoped."[92]

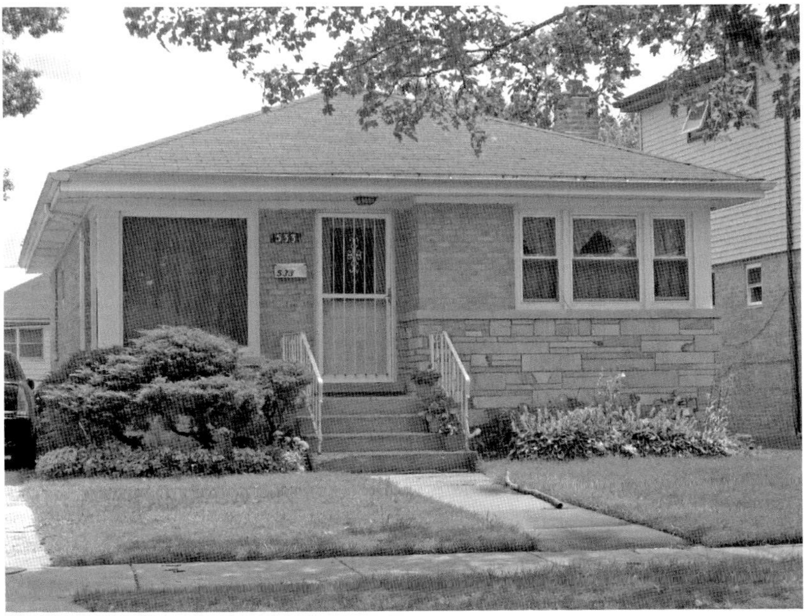

John Nagle's former house in Bellwood, where his family gathered to mourn his death and the tragic events of October 27, 1967. *Photo taken by Edgar Gamboa Návar.*

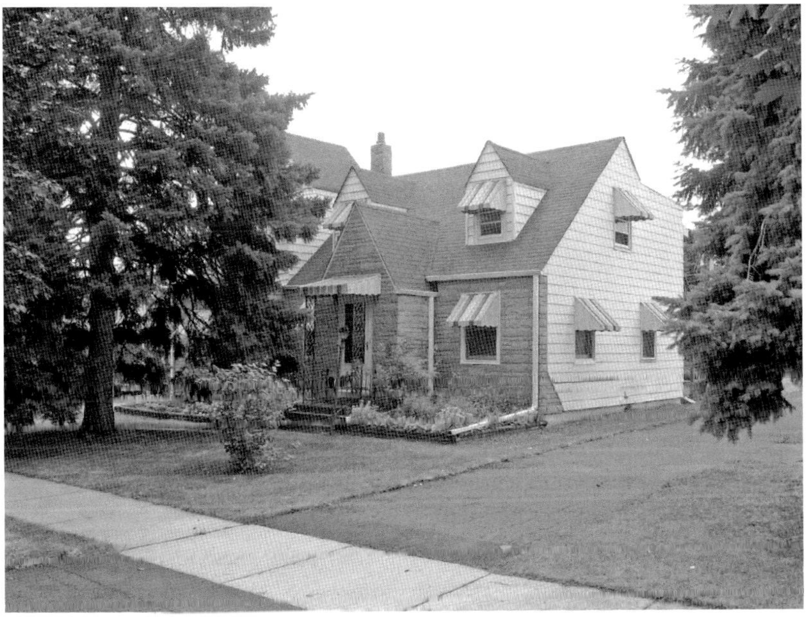

The former Perri home sits near the center of Northlake, just a few blocks from Nagle-Perri Park. The Perri family gathered in this home to mourn Anthony's death. *Photo taken by Edgar Gamboa Návar.*

At the Villa Scalabrini Old People's Home, Antoinette, dressed in her white nurse's aide uniform, fulfilled her daily responsibilities. She didn't realize that across the street from her work three gunmen used a public phone that diverted the police force and led to her husband's ambush attack.

A police car pulled into the parking lot. The policeman stepped out of the car and headed for the Villa Scalabrini entrance. The receptionist told the officer she would look for Antoinette. She was found tending to a resident. The feeling in her stomach sank as her co-worker told her a police officer was here to talk to her. Her thoughts quickly ran into the various possibilities of what could be wrong—from one of her kids to her husband. The officer pulled her aside and told her that her husband had been shot and killed. She sobbed uncontrollably as she wailed, "No more, Tony! No more, Tony!"[93] Her knees slightly buckled as the officer grabbed her arm and held her up.

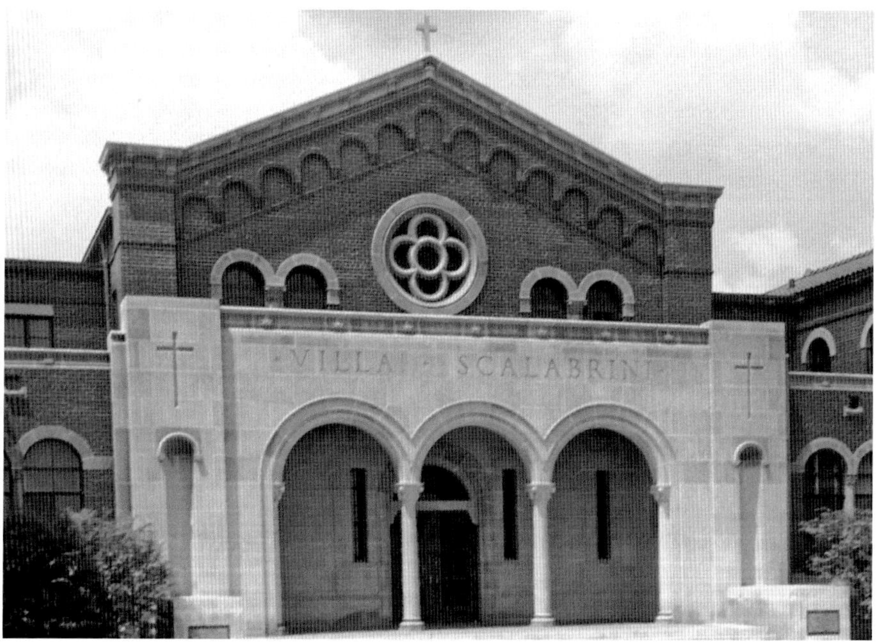

Villa Scalabrini is the place where Anthony Perri dropped off his wife, Antoinette, the morning of the shooting. *Courtesy of Villa Scalabrini.*

OCTOBER 27, 1967

SUSPECTS

Although Chief Gilliam refused to name them as accomplices, the Stewarts were people of interest, and this early in the investigation every morsel of information was invaluable to them. There was a possibility that the two remaining bandits were hiding in their home—or, at the very least, that they received aid from them. Witnesses repeated seeing a woman drive the getaway car from the factory. As the FBI trimmed down the list of potential suspects, local authorities did their own groundwork as they searched for the names Raine gave them.

The police issued a radio bulletin for James and Deborah Stewart. Law enforcement personnel realized other agencies also wanted them. Deborah worked as a waitress at a popular local restaurant, the Come Back Inn in Melrose Park. There, another waitress, Joy O'Quinn, said she was Deborah's former roommate and fellow server. O'Quinn quickly told them that Deborah's husband, James, was going to be sent to Kentucky as a parole violator. She gave a quick description of his appearance. He found work at a Northlake factory but was caught stealing from a soda machine at work. The police fervently looked for both of them. Gilliam, however, wasn't too sure there was a legitimate connection between this crime and the Stewarts.[94]

FBI AGENTS DILIGENTLY searched their own national database. Their initial step included compiling a list of persons capable of such a crime. High-powered weapons were recently used in other crimes, serving as a clue. They recovered the slugs found on the scene and sent them to the proper science labs. The .351 automatic rifle left outside the bank served as the biggest clue—those casings belonged to that rifle. Cross-referencing the bullets with other crimes took time.

In the meantime, three names came up time and again. Only a few persons were capable of such a crime. The first name was Henry Michael Gargano. The second name was Clifton Orneal Daniels. And the third name was confirmed as the person captured: Ronald Dale Raine. All three had served time together in a federal penitentiary. Relationships were established there. The next step matched the blood found in the abandoned vehicle with the blood of the two suspected fugitives. That verified their hunches.

AS THE MONEY scattered outside the bank was collected, stored and appropriately marked, the FBI intently asked the witnesses every detail that concerned the ordeal that lasted under two minutes. They asked about the appearance of the bandits and the length of the robbery; other questions concerned the customers themselves—what was their business in the bank that day?

The team lifted fingerprints all over the bank as they made every effort to finalize a list of possible perpetrators. They also determined the amount the thieves took:

$83,783.45 was the total amount taken from the tellers' cages.
$5,600 was recovered outside the Northlake Bank, loot dropped by the bandits.
$200 was found in the bloodied getaway car.[95]

That left $77, 983.45 unaccounted for, money that needed to be recovered.

THE REMAINDER OF THE day at the crime scene included an entourage of reporters gathering to cover the day's top news. They questioned neighbors, did their own searches and gathered vital information to tell the story of the grisly scene. To the press, they formed part of the team in providing the solution and did not see themselves as the problem. They informed the public, creating greater chances of apprehending the perpetrators. By providing critical information to the public, the press saw themselves as an additional avenue in solving the case. Press reporters assiduously assembled the morning's events, noting the weapons used, the bloody vehicle found less than a mile away, the shell casing and bodies on the ground—relaying it all back to their news stations and media centers for dispersion to the public. Radio stations instantly picked up the story, reporting it to their audiences.

As for the local community, the end of October 27, 1967, brought the confirmation of two deceased police officers. Local law enforcement agencies thought it best to enhance their chances at capturing these culprits by working as a single cohesive unit. Their next steps were to focus on the manhunt and apprehension of these despised bandits. They were to act quickly and decisively.

Chapter 3

OCTOBER 28–29, 1967

The Manhunt

Clues

The FBI agents' national effort proved fruitful as the culprits were identified and confirmed. Investigators took blood samples from the abandoned Buick Skylark left outside the factory parking lot. The trace to Daniels didn't demonstrate a match. Gargano's blood match, however, did return as positive. Officer Bartkavich certainly hit Gargano in the arm. Now the FBI gathered more information on the culprits and pieced together this puzzle that seemed archaic but provided relevant clues.

According to Marlin Johnson, head of the Chicago FBI office, the main guy behind the shooting was Henry Michael Gargano. Gargano was born in Chicago; measured five feet, eleven inches; weighed 175 pounds; and had brown hair. He had recently been released from the federal penitentiary in downstate Marion, Illinois, about a five-hour drive from Chicago, in March 1967. Reason for time served: bank robbery. He had a penchant for violent crimes. Since he had served time for a bank robbery, the FBI was not surprised to see his name associated with this grisly event. He had done it before, and now he had struck again. Gargano tasted the thrill of robbing a bank, shot to kill and attempted to get away with it. He had lasted a little more than six months out of prison before he returned to a life of crime—just six months! As the authorities investigated further, they soon realized that a crime gang had pulled off a series of robberies throughout the Midwest.

As the FBI initially gathered Gargano's record, they were astonished at what they discovered:

1946: Convicted for burglary; sentenced to a reformatory.
1949: Armed robbery; sentenced one to three years.
1952: Convicted for armed robbery; sentenced to two to four years.
1956: Convicted for bank robbery; sentenced to eighteen years in the penitentiary.
1964: Convicted for escape from prison; sentenced to three years.

After Gargano's list of crimes was gathered, the FBI was mesmerized that such a man had freedom. Since his first incident as a teenager, Gargano had been sentenced to some form of incarceration for more time than time spent as a free person. His life of defying authorities and engaging in criminal acts had started out as a teenager. His list of robberies included armed robbery. He proved his displeasure for authority with his escape from prison. There was little doubt that Gargano was the leader of such a unit. His temperament and attitude were natural traits that helped him run a crime gang by example. As the FBI investigated further, they uncovered more pieces to the puzzle. They needed to find out where the crime gang obtained military weapons—after all, these were the type of guns the U.S. military used in the Vietnam War. These weapons did not belong in the hands of formerly convicted criminals.

The FBI quickly disclosed the other name: Clifton Orneal Daniels. Daniels was born and reared in Cisne, Illinois, a village downstate in proximity to St. Louis rather than Chicago. He was five feet, five and a half inches tall, weighed 145 pounds and had brown hair. Daniels had been discharged the previous January. Just like Gargano, his time served in the federal penitentiary of Marion was for bank robbery. And just like Gargano, he lasted less than a year out of prison before he returned to what he liked best: bank robberies.

After further research, records revealed Daniels's long criminal record:

1956: Convicted of attempted larceny; sentenced to six months in jail.
1957: Convicted of carrying a concealed weapon; fined.
1958: Kidnapping and auto theft; sentenced to youth commission.
1961: Convicted for bank robbery; sentenced to fifteen years.

Daniels's criminal record extended over twenty years. Although he did not have a record for murder, theft seemed to be his crime of desire. His past revealed kidnapping and vehicle theft, and he had served time for bank robbery. Further investigation was required, but his experience in stealing cars was a vital skill to have in this profession. Gangs needed getaway cars, and they needed to be undetected.

Bullet Casings, Matches and a Robbery in Ohio

Forensic experts at the crime scene gathered the bullet casings, packaging them to be properly examined. They desired to gather as much information as possible, realizing that an expedited process served to their advantage. Once they packaged the critical evidence, they shipped the bullet casing to the ballistics department under FBI authority. The FBI wanted to look for possible matches in previous crimes in order to link these bandits with any other robbery in the area. A rash of bank robberies had occurred in the Chicago area in previous months, and solving these events with a possible common thread would prove efficient.

Unfortunately, after examining the shell casings, negative connections were made to these Chicago robberies. However, the pellets retrieved at the Northlake Bank did result in a match. That match was not in Chicago, though. Results confirmed a match with pellets retrieved at another shootout in which high-powered weapons were used. Furthermore, FBI investigators matched the automatic rifle recovered in Northlake to a previous crime in Canton, Ohio, several weeks earlier. Initial assumptions led to the FBI linking these brash bandits with the Canton thieves. The Chicago FBI office quickly contacted its Ohio branch counterparts to compare more evidence with the purpose of further confirming the bandits at both scenes.

After properly collaborating, the Ohio FBI agents informed their Chicago counterparts of the events that had happened several weeks prior to the Northlake Bank robbery so that they would better understand the subjects of their manhunt. If Gargano and Daniels were indeed behind both robberies and subsequent shootouts, then these men not only enjoyed possessing high-powered weapons, but they also enjoyed aiming them at police officers. The Canton, Ohio robbery struck fear in law enforcement.

A total of fifty bullets had been recovered from the wild shootout that took place in Canton, Ohio, on October 13, 1967.[96] The FBI had investigated that case and thought the gang would strike again. By the looks of the initial investigation into the Northlake robbery, this gang was more than just a few guys who robbed stores and banks. They had been a larger group—probably a network of ex-cons—that strung together a series of robberies. Immediately, police started to question whether this gang of bandits had gone on a weekend rampage since similar shootings were reported in Michigan, Kentucky, Indiana and Illinois. They had work to do to make those connections.

On the corner of Mahoning Avenue and Meridian Road in quaint Canton, Ohio, sat the Mahoning Road Plaza. The plaza consisted of a variety of stores, such as a barbershop, a Western Auto store and an A&P store. The neighborhood was typically quiet and safe. Construction began in August 1954, and the shopping center was completed in March 1955 on the site of the old McKinley Airport.[97] The 1950s provided growth for Canton, incorporated as a city in 1838. As wealthier citizens moved to the suburbs, shopping was done at suburban shopping centers instead of downtown. Like many other cities across America, Canton experienced a postwar economic boom. The need for these shopping centers was evident—and these towns built them.

Crimes had occurred in Canton, but no armed robberies that involved high-powered weapons. And certainly, no shootings that involved Canton police. A Canton police officer had not been shot since policeman Earl "Red" Acker in 1948 after he attempted to foil a robbery attempt. He was shot in the stomach and survived. All of that changed on Friday, October 13, 1967. This midwestern city of 110,000 was shaken to its core.

Four men, working together, had decided to rob a local supermarket during busy hours. They figured to go in the store quietly, rob the store and get out as soon as possible without detection. Although they had access to machine guns, their intention was not to use them. But if things got messy, they didn't hesitate to shoot to kill. The four men, police had later discovered, were Henry Gargano, Clifton Daniels, Ronald Dale Raine and Ralph Garduno. To pull off the robbery, they had used a getaway vehicle. That Friday afternoon, they used Garduno's car to approach a factory parking lot in the northeast section of town. The Republic Steel Corporation employed many local residents, and during the second shift their cars remained unattended. Clifton Daniels and the others broke into a 1963 Buick vehicle without hesitation and without being noticed. All four men rode off in two cars, ready for their brazen attempt later that night.

Shortly after 7:00 p.m., two men had entered the A&P store while it was full of customers. Daniels, who had worn a baseball cap, was one of the men. He had kept his head slightly tilted downward and to the right with both hands in his jacket. He was shorter in stature than his accomplice. The other man, Gargano, had walked more upright as if he displayed greater confidence. He had a more serious demeanor. Both men, however, walked into the store seemingly indistinguishable from the other customers.

The unnoticed men had quickly walked past customers as they paid for items and approached the produce manager. The bandits told the manager that they were robbing the store. The two robbers briskly walked the produce manager to the store office, briefly showing him the butt of Daniels's weapon and telling the head cashier of their plan to take the money from the cash registers. As the head cashier cashed checks and handled money orders, she mentioned that the safe sitting on the floor contained no money. She did some quick thinking since the safe deposit box did contain more cash. She had all the money for the evening in her hands, she explained in hopes of stalling them. Meanwhile, customers went about their business as they shopped and exited the store without a hint of what was transpiring.

One of the robbers had stood waiting for his accomplice near a book rack at the west end of the store. The other thief waited and stared at the head cashier and informed her to remove all of the cash from each of the six cash registers. She was not to try anything funny or she and the customers might be hurt; she was simply to do as told.

Meanwhile, in the few moments that they waited, a customer paid for her items. She asked for a dime as change. She then walked out of the store and noticed the odd man present. It seemed to her that he was up to no good. Without looking back and without making a commotion, this customer briskly walked out of the store, picked up the local public telephone and notified police of her observations as her heart beat faster at what she thought was certainly a robbery. Because she had walked smoothly out of the store, she went unnoticed. The police never identified the caller.

The bandits had gathered $3,500 from the A&P store as they walked out. The money was stuffed in a brown paper bag. Daniels carried the bag with a tight-clenched fist. One bandit briskly walked toward a 1963 Buick, and the other bandit walked near the barbershop toward another vehicle. There were a total of four bandits with two vehicles. Suddenly, a police car swiftly approached the store through the parking lot. The robbery became more interesting.

The evening shift had begun like any other workday for Canton patrolmen Earl E. Schoeneman and Nick David Nitzu. A Canton police veteran for over six years, Patrolman Schoeneman was a father to five children. Now thirty-five years of age, he enjoyed being a cop. Serving Canton residents was a privilege for him. He wanted to be a cop for as long as he could. His partner, Nick David Nitzu, was a little younger—in experience and age. Patrolman Nitzu was twenty-eight years old, a father to fourteen-month-old Lisa Ann and husband to Anita, who was expecting their second child. As he eagerly looked forward to becoming a father for the second time, Nitzu dominated the conversation while on patrol with Schoeneman. All he had talked about was becoming a dad again.

Both Patrolmen Schoeneman and Nitzu were engrossed in a conversation as they cruised the northeast section of town when the call came in over the radio. There was a robbery in process at the Mahoning Avenue Plaza. That was only a few minutes away. As they headed to the plaza, Patrolman Nitzu noticed one man with a ball cap clutching a brown paper bag.

"Earl! That's our man!"[98]

Schoeneman suggested they approach slowly. The man with the brown bag "began to walk faster" toward them.[99]

Daniels wore a ball cap. He brandished his weapon as he pulled out a gun and shot at the police cruiser, striking Schoeneman. As Schoeneman groaned from the wound, Nitzu crouched in his seat as he attempted to avoid any gunshots fired in his direction. He eventually dropped his gun on the floor. Opening the door, he realized that his partner was now wounded—and was lying facedown on the pavement. The bandit's brazen attempt raced through Nitzu's mind. He wondered if he would see his children again. After a brief break in the shooting, Nitzu stepped out of the cruiser, crouched, lunged toward his revolver, recovered it and aimed at Daniels. Nitzu fired "five times through the cruiser's windshield at him and then all hell broke loose."[100] Nitzu recognized the high-powered weapons Daniels's accomplices possessed as glass flew everywhere. He reached for his police radio as bullets penetrated the police cruiser.

A bullet struck Nitzu in the back. Daniels approached the car to aim better at the policemen. "Daniels walked around the cruiser and fired into the cruiser and at Schoeneman."[101] Daniels ran toward one of the getaway vehicles. The police cruiser's other windows were shattered, leaving shards of glass everywhere. Their car continuously took heavy fire.

As that took place, Gargano ran west in the parking lot toward a 1963 Buick as an additional gunman had waited near the vehicle. That gunman felt threatened as the police cruiser fired at them and engaged the policemen with high-powered rifles. The bullet holes on the cruiser were later traced to these machine guns. The gunman in the 1963 Buick quickly had driven toward the barbershop, and Daniels jumped in. Ralph Garduno had driven the other car that was also engaged in the shootout before it left the scene. In total, all four gunmen had hit the police cruiser with twenty-one shots that penetrated the left and front side of the car. The patrolmen's revolvers simply were no match for the bandit's assault weapons. The car looked as if it had been through a war zone.

Just as quickly as the shooting had started, it ended. The bandits took off northbound and then eastward as they drove away in a white Buick from the Mahoning Plaza Shopping Center and into a residential area. Some boys hanging out at the plaza saw them last. The bandits were gone—at least for the moment. Hope remained that the culprits would be captured. There were too many witnesses who could identify the getaway cars.

The scene was reminiscent of Chicago's Al Capone, something Canton residents hoped remained in the big cities, away from quiet midsized towns such as Canton. Canton police chief Frank Burnosky raced to the scene and issued orders for all area cops to block any arterial escapes out of town in an effort to apprehend the culprits. The more quickly their fellow officers responded, the greater their chances at catching the shooters. Chief Burnosky also issued a seven-state alarm to notify police departments in surrounding states. He wanted everyone to be on the lookout for bandits with high-powered weapons. Roadblocks were temporarily set up in such places as Calhoun County in southern Michigan—the next confirmed sighting of the bandits.

Chief Burnosky felt disturbed by the scene in front of him—Patrolman Nitzu had suffered from a single gunshot wound to the back. He lay on the ground in pain as he grimaced. Patrolman Schoeneman was in agony from four shots. Chief Burnosky had known these two patrolmen well—Nitzu had valiantly served the police department since 1965, and Schoeneman had served since 1961. They were both good and faithful officers. Schoeneman had suffered from several wounds—to the groin, left leg, left shoulder and right side. Both men would undergo surgery and recover from their wounds.

Chief Burnosky had scanned the crime scene around him, perplexed as to the motive and the number of shell casings before his eyes. He counted up to ten shell casings in his vicinity. He picked up one, examined it and determined it came from a high-powered .45-caliber automatic weapon.

The incident had terrified Chief Burnosky. His mind raced as to the perpetrators.

Authorities later identified the driver of a getaway vehicle as Ralph Garduno of Akron, Ohio. As he drove away from the plaza, Garduno and the others escaped arrest. He was present at the A&P store shooting and then drove another vehicle besides the primary stolen car that witnesses later identified. That car received two bullet holes, and the culprits abandoned it soon thereafter. Police found the abandoned car later that day. Garduno's car, however, was also identified at the scene because of a single shot that penetrated his vehicle. After the gang dispersed later that day, Garduno went about his daily business. He thought he was safe. After all, he simply provided backup to the two men inside the store. Garduno remained calm.

The following day, on October 14, Garduno awoke and started to go about his daily business. His car had been spotted parked on a side street in the area. The Canton police sat waiting for someone to enter the vehicle. Garduno walked slowly toward the car, cautiously looked around for marked police cars, and didn't notice anything extraordinary. As Garduno opened the door ready to get in the car, police ambushed him and arrested him. Garduno had been captured. He'd agreed to do this job to make some money, he stated. His responsibility included providing needed backup to his companion. Canton police felt some justice, as they had apprehended one of the henchmen. The other members of the gang remained free, at least for the moment.

Gargano, Raine and Daniels had left the Canton area soon after they parted ways with Garduno. They needed to be continuously on the move if they were to return to Chicago undetected. Cops usually issued alerts and radio reports to fellow officers soon after such incidents occurred. Police were on the lookout for them. They had decided to take a circuitous route back to Chicago as they traveled through southern Michigan near Interstate 94. They headed north toward Ann Arbor, Michigan, away from Ohio before going west to Chicago. They were spotted at about 10:00 p.m. on Friday night near Marshall, Michigan, after driving for a few hours.

Sergeant Crook of the Marshall Police Department was working the night shift when he spotted a car that matched the description of a possible vehicle involved in the Canton, Ohio shooting a few hours earlier. The car was a 1956 Ford. Crooks noticed a unique feature of the car: "a dog with blinking lights for eyes used to signal turns."[102] Sergeant Crooks immediately followed the car and radioed to a fellow unit about the incident. A second police car joined the chase. The bandits' car eventually reached almost one hundred miles per hour. Suddenly, one of the bandits stuck his head out of the window and fired at the trailing officers with a machine gun to thwart the pursuers. Sergeant Crooks returned a single shot that failed to hit its target. The bandits had fired once more and forced the pursuing vehicles to slow down. That's when the 1956 Ford made a turn into a side road off M-60 as it sped into the darkness and eventually disappeared from the pursuing police officers.

And so it was that a few weeks later in Northlake, Illinois, the match had been made. The weapon used in the Canton, Ohio shooting was the same weapon used to rob the Northlake Bank. In both instances, a high-powered machine gun was used, shooting .351-caliber bullets. The FBI quickly matched a .351 cartridge recovered in Canton with the weapon used in Northlake. The Winchester automatic weapon found in Northlake was the same weapon used in Canton. Further analysis revealed that a .45 cartridge fired in Canton came from the same gun that lay near Raine in Northlake. Ballistic tests revealed the validity of their hunches. These were the same perpetrators who struck fear into the Canton community and wounded two Canton police officers.

Without hesitation, the FBI Cleveland office issued a federal warrant for the arrest of Clifton Orneal Daniels and Henry Michael Gargano since they had fled Ohio in an attempt to avoid prosecution for armed robbery. This group of bandits was now wanted in two states for two grisly crimes—both were robberies, and both involved viciously shooting policemen with intent to kill. Canton police officer Nitzu later admitted that the shooters were intent on killing them. "They didn't want to just wound or scare us; they fully intended to kill us," Nitzu commented.[103]

The Search

Northlake police chief Gilliam questioned both James and Deborah Stewart, trying to garner more information on the two fugitives. The more quickly they learned all they could about their past and their plans, the more quickly this whole nightmare would come to an end. Gilliam's investigative suspicions were correct: they were not connected with this particular crime. Evidence simply did not point in their direction. Although they possibly had a relationship with the bandits, they were not associates—at least not this time. Specifically, Deborah wasn't the driver in the getaway car spotted by witnesses. Their names were crossed off the list.[104] But if Deborah Stewart was not the driver, then who was? A woman was definitely seen in the vehicle by witnesses. Northlake police canvassed the area in addition to their day-to-day operations. There was no time to stop the essential police work that needed to take place.

As local law enforcement proceeded with local canvassing, the FBI agents searched their databases to gather leads as they determined the inner workings of the crime gang. The FBI interviewed prisoners at Marion to determine with whom the bandits had established relationships during their prison time. Gargano and Daniels had been released from prison earlier that year—in March 1967, to be specific. Raine spent a little more time out of prison than both of them, but he continued with his life of crime. After they linked the two crimes in Northlake and Canton, the FBI grew curious about similar actions taken throughout the region. They searched for crimes in which similar weapons were used. The FBI compiled an internal list of possible accomplices. In their research, Henry Gargano was the likely leader of this crime syndicate.

Besides, Gargano, Raine and Daniels had served prison terms in Marion Federal Penitentiary together. Their prisoner numbers A-247, A-243 and A-284 proved their imprisonment together at Marion starting on August 6, 1964. Marion was notorious for housing dangerous inmates. Soon they added the names of three prolific bank robbers as former residents.

The wounded Gargano, his sister Annette and Daniels spent Friday night restless and anxious. Annette managed to successfully stop the bleeding from Gargano's shoulder, and they got some needed rest that night. They spent all day Friday and through the night with the windows opened. Gargano insisted they remain open in case cops showed up. He ordered Daniels to bring some weapons from one of the bedroom closets and place them near the windows. Daniels placed some rifles and guns near the windows. They were loaded and ready to be fired. Gargano refused to surrender without putting up a fight. He insisted they keep the windows open and that they shoot if any cops asked for them. Gargano made sure Daniels knew proper protocol: always shoot to kill.

On Saturday at 7:30 a.m., the three ventured to their next stop. Raine had been caught, and he would likely divert the cops as long as possible, but fingerprints would ultimately identify Gargano and Daniels as the additional gunmen. They had to move and move quickly. Besides, the blood drips that led up to the apartment created concern, certainly with the owner downstairs or at least with some of the neighbors. Gargano insisted on going to his girlfriend's apartment in the city, near the lake. Once they picked her up they could go anywhere from there. Daniels helped Gargano down the stairs and into the backseat of the 1967 Ford owned by Raine. The car was parked in the dilapidated garage, and it leaned to the right. Annette sat in the front seat in an attempt to avoid suspicion. As Daniels's nerves slightly rattled him, he looked at the shelf on the inside garage door. Sitting on top was the Coffee Mate jar he had placed there a few weeks ago when everything seemed so thrilling. His brief moment of reflection passed, and his glance now turned to his companions and fellow fugitives. He entered the driver seat as the chauffer. Now, there was an additional accomplice.

The 606 Club

Sex in the 1960s was prevalent. The country was at war, both externally and internally. Divisions existed on whether to support the war, support our troops or simply support the freedom of sex in the counterculture movement. For returning soldiers from war, the entertainment provided included visiting clubs that offered striptease shows. Transitioning away from striptease shows moved along at a frenetic pace. The industry changed itself into something much more. The sex entertainment industry was initially built primarily on "teasing" the audience. Creating a sensualized experience had been the norm, but not anymore. Entertainment was now based more on stripping and hard-core pornography so that getting up close and personal was the choice of many male customers. Instead of sitting at tables mesmerized by entertainers, the audience was encouraged to sit close to the dancers. There was a center stage with a catwalk that brought the dancers to the audience for a more personalized experience. And "teasing" was replaced with stripping.

As for Chicago, the scene was no different than in other American cities. People moved to the big city for work and for greater opportunities. As a result, businesses grew. And so did entertainment directed exclusively at men. Strip nightclubs opened, many along Madison Street, such as the L&L Café. The South Loop wasn't too far behind, especially with the Chicago and the

National, two of the better-known clubs and more frequented locations. As a result, businesses grew.

On the 600 block of Wabash stood a popular club that "encouraged its patrons to sit close to the performers and drink beer."[105] That place was called the 606 Club.[106] The bar was in the rear of the place, the stage was in the front and in between the two were tables for customers to sit and enjoy seeing the performers.[107]

One of their better-known performers in 1967 was a dancer named Sheer Folly. Her blond hair and curves drew the attention of many customers. She had a loyal clientele base—and one of those customers was Henry Gargano. Gargano initiated a relationship with her, as he was mesmerized by her looks and movement on stage. She struck a feeling in him.

The feeling was mutual. She was drawn to him—he was confident, he was adventurous and he lived an exciting life. The manner in which he smoked cigarettes and looked at her performing on stage separated him from the others. Gargano soon learned that her real name was Monica Florence Conner.[108] She was a divorcée and a native Texan.

Monica lived on Bellevue Place, off Rush Street, in the city's uptown section. Daniels drove to Monica's apartment on Bellevue Place, using the Eisenhower Expressway built the previous decade to serve the communities that surrounded Bellwood and now aptly served them.

Daniels dropped off Annette at Monica's apartment as they hoped to rest there. Annette quickly walked up the stairs and knocked on Monica's door at around 7:30 a.m. Annette introduced herself and then asked her if she would let Gargano come in. She shared with her that he was hurt.

"I do not want him in my apartment," Monica stated.[109]

"He wants to talk to you," Annette quickly answered.[110]

"I'll let him come up if you stay, Annette," was Monica's answer.[111]

With Daniels's help, Gargano walked gingerly as he clutched his shoulder to ease the throbbing pain that continued and entered Monica's apartment, 1-C. Daniels then drove the Ford to the parking lot on the back side of the apartment. After parking there, Daniels ran up the stairs with a suitcase in hand and knocked on the apartment door.[112] Monica answered the door, still shocked by the scene she had seen as Gargano's blood stained his shirt.

Annette rushed into the bathroom as thoughts returned to her mind about her brother and his troubles. To have a brother in jail was one thing, as was the case with Michael Salvatore Gargano. However, to lose a brother was completely different. Henry almost lost his life. No matter what Henry did, she felt close to him. She took the glass in the bathroom, filled it with water and sipped it. She then left the bathroom, walked over to the dining area and drew the brown-colored ashtray closer to her. She thought that all she needed was a smoke. A cigarette would calm her nerves, so she grabbed one from her purse, lit it and took a drag in hopes the surreal moment would disappear and she would be home with her father and kids a long way from here, in Bolingbrook.

Gargano saw the acetone bottle in the dining area. Annette walked over, grabbed it and attempted to clean his wound as best as possible.

"He was badly wounded in the right upper arm," Monica said to herself.[113]

Annette then mentioned to Monica that Gargano was badly shot. Annette and Monica cleaned the wound and tried to stop the bleeding. "After we got Gargano comfortable in a bed, I asked him when he had been wounded and he told me that it happened yesterday."[114]

Monica then asked Gargano "if he had robbed the bank yesterday."[115]

Gargano replied, "We were the ones."[116] He then mentioned that the police caught Raine at the bank.

Gargano winced in pain. Daniels told them Gargano needed medical attention, but giving themselves up was not an option—anything but that. They had no intentions of returning to prison. Escape was the only path they would take—either that or go down fighting. Daniels placed the suitcase on the dining area counter where they had gathered. He turned his attention to Monica, opened the suitcase and pulled out $5,000 in cash as he gave it to her and commanded her to get some kind of assistance from a doctor—a doctor who could be bribed to keep his mouth shut. Someone should be able to suture the wound.[117] Discretion continued to be of utmost importance.

By now the police department had likely identified them and set up teams to canvass the area. The news bulletins over the radio were a detriment to their escape. Everyone with access to television or radio already knew about the Northlake Bank robbery. Media picked up the story quickly. Staying in Chicago was not an option. They had to get out. Daniels listened as Annette smoked her cigarette, paced the area back and forth and thought about her children.

After she grabbed the cash, Monica put the money in her purse. As she made an effort to find medical help, the others' conversation turned to their next move. Gargano, the group's strongest personality, suggested they stick together and leave the city as he grabbed the Camel cigarette pack to have a smoke. A cigarette eased his nerves and allowed him to think. Gargano's strength was just enough to smoke a cigarette.

Monica told them of a doctor on the South Side who might help. She then "went to a Dr. Howard's office on 63rd Street."[118] She thought he might help since "he was a colored doctor."[119] Besides, Monica had "known that Dr. Howard was an abortionist."[120]

ON THE SOUTH SIDE of Chicago, Dr. Theodore Roosevelt Mason Howard readied himself in his clinic to meet the medical needs of the day. This Saturday morning, he received a silver-blond woman with an odd request. He was used to many oddities in his life since he was engaged in the civil rights movement and its many facets. He had even helped with the Emmett Till murder investigation years ago. He learned to maintain the course with his convictions as he voiced strong opposition to socialism—not a popular position among his peers. After all, there was a movement toward socialist ideals—the 1960s, he thought. He was again forced to make a choice.

Monica Conner jumped into a cab, which took Lake Shore Drive to visit the African American doctor. He was their best chance to fix Gargano's shoulder. As the cab drove, she looked out into the beautiful waters of Lake Michigan on her left. The lake's strong waves crashed into the walls that served as a barrier between the waves and the street she currently rode on. The waves' sound had served as tranquility for her many times over as she walked along the shoreline during periods of nice weather. Monica thought today was not one of those days. The snow that fell the day before didn't provide that serenity. The rush of adrenaline she experienced didn't provide that serenity either as her apartment was full of fugitives. She quickly snaked her way along the towering buildings of Chicago's downtown as she left them behind, heading toward Chicago's South Side in hopes of finding help.

At 555 East Sixty-third Street, Dr. Howard noticed the blond woman walking into his clinic. She seemed distressed and in a rush.

Dr. Howard asked her in what way he could be of help. Monica replied that she needed help for her brother.

Dr. Howard demanded that she tell him exactly the help her brother needed. Dr. Howard simply reiterated to her that he could not be of help unless she was honest with him.

Monica quickly retorted that she wanted him to help her brother out. She said that her brother was a parolee and had been shot. Monica reasoned logically that she couldn't take him to the hospital since he was a parolee. She just wanted him to look at his wound.

Monica just wanted to find help, and hopefully the difficult situation would pass soon. Gargano brought excitement to her life—but this was flat-out dangerous, she reasoned to herself.

Skeptical, Dr. Howard seemed guarded. Monica promptly pulled out the suitcase and told him, "I'll give you $5,000 in cash to disinfect the wound and suture it!"[121]

Dr. Howard thought for a second. Given his own legal problems at the moment, he felt pulled in two directions. His medical side wanted to help this man out, but helping a parolee brought more legal troubles. Dr. Howard had been convicted of income tax evasion for accepting $500 in marked bills to perform an abortion. In his eyes, he was doing the right thing. According to the government, his crime was not reporting the income.[122]

Dr. Howard reasoned with Monica and told her that he lamented being unable to help her brother out. Dr. Howard, however, was willing to give her pain medication.

Dr. Howard walked toward the dispensary and grabbed some pills. As he walked back to the woman once more, he thought of the person's identity. Nothing crossed his mind—and rightly so, since not everyone was aware of the bank robbery that had taken place the day before—but if that man was a parolee, then he was bad news.

Monica insisted one last time that if the doctor helped them out, she would give him $20,000 in cash, in addition to the $5,000 he would receive at the moment.

Dr. Howard demanded that she be honest with him.

Monica came clean. She told Dr. Howard that it wasn't her brother who was hurt. It was her boyfriend, and he was involved in a bank robbery. All she was trying to do was find him some help. That's all!

He told her once more that all he would be able to do is give her fifteen capsules of over-the-counter pain killers. That's it. Nothing more. Monica walked out of the office, showed her appreciation and was still in despair.

She got in her cab and traveled back to her apartment with the capsules and no medical doctor to assist. She hoped Gargano would understand. As she left the doctor's office, she pulled out a cigarette, lit it and hoped her nerves would calm down.

Dr. Howard still thought about his own legal issues as he called the state's attorney's office and told them about his early morning encounter. Dr. Howard reiterated to them, "I did not accept any money from those people whatsoever, and I want to make that clear."[123]

A Check for Each Widow

The vicious events at the Northlake Bank shocked the civic organizations that soon united to meet necessary financial needs. The One Hundred Club was established in 1956 to assist the dependents of policemen and firemen killed in the line of duty. Within twenty-four hours, the One Hundred Club presented the widows of fallen policemen and firemen with $1,000 checks. The One Hundred Club went beyond meeting needs—they took the necessary steps to pay for the remaining mortgage and any outstanding debt.

Local club president Ralph Scheu quickly took the initiative to present Marlene Nagle, wife of fallen officer John J. Nagle, with her $1,000 check. Marlene Nagle, grateful for the gift, accepted it thinking she would have rather never been put in a position to receive the check. The other mourning widow, Antoinette Perri, was not present due to the anxiety of losing her husband. She remained under a physician's care, completely distraught by the fact that she would no longer hear her husband sing those Italian songs joyfully. She was not present at the Northlake Police Station to receive her check. Arrangements were later made for her. Her Tony was gone, forever.

Warrants and Charges

Wasting little time, the FBI rapidly addressed the robbery as it charged the culprits. The Cleveland office of the FBI charged Clifton Orneal Daniels and Henry Michael Gargano with unlawful flight to avoid arrest in connection with the October 13 supermarket robbery in Canton, Ohio. Murder charges were not filed—at least not in that case. Besides, according to federal law, only local law enforcement could place murder charges. So the only person on this Saturday afternoon charged with murder was Ronald Dale Raine.

Local officials swiftly approached a judge in felony court to place the necessary charges. With the charges, both local and federal officials were authorized to seek and arrest the perpetrators for specific crimes. Judge Daniel J. Ryan in felony court granted the state permission to file murder charges against Raine. The FBI followed that charge as it issued federal warrants for the Northlake robbery for both Gargano and Daniels. Federal authorities and local authorities worked closely together, confident that they would apprehend the bandits. The bandits' evasiveness could last for only so long. Northlake police chief Gilliam publicly and confidently stated on Monday night, October 30, that "the search for Gargano and Daniels will be over within 24 hours."[124]

Gargano and Annette convinced Monica to join them. They were going away for a few days until things settled down a bit. Monica grappled with staying behind and simply ending the relationship with Gargano, something she had unsuccessfully tried several times—but he simply wouldn't let her go. Monica told them that she needed to talk with her employer first at the 606 Club. She didn't want to lose her job. That job was her primary source of income.

As Monica went to the club, she questioned her decision to join Gargano, Daniels and Annette. That was a risky move, she thought. There was no reason for her to do that—but Gargano and others knew her. If she decided not to join them and Gargano was caught, his network of friends would surely single her out. Monica needed the extra money they paid for her services. In many ways, she needed to satisfy her customer base. In many other ways, these relationships exceeded her job responsibilities. Her relationship with clients such as Gargano provided the means for her to live in the Gold Coast and maintain the lifestyle she now was accustomed to living. They were criminals, but they also paid very well.

Monica entered the club, walked over to the club manager and explained to him that she was going to miss the next few days of work.[125] Her mother in Texas was ill, and she was going to visit her. Her boss, knowing that Monica attracted a customer base, offered to make plane reservations for her or to use the company card to pay for the flight. Monica was visibly upset, thanked her boss for the nice gestures and walked briskly out of the club as tears rolled down her cheeks.

Monica's dilemma of joining Gargano and the others ended. She made the choice to join them. The result of this decision was unknown. Monica returned to her apartment, notified another friend who worked as a barmaid nearby and told her that she would be gone for a few days visiting her sick mother in Texas. The deal was done. She assisted Annette with Gargano's ailing shoulder and became a fellow fugitive of the Northlake Bank robbers.

On Saturday night, Gargano, Daniels, Monica and Annette were again on the move. At approximately 11:00 p.m., Daniels drove the 1967 green-colored Ford to a nearby parking lot located at 1037 North Rush Street. It was Saturday night, and many people were leaving restaurants to go to bars and clubs in the area. He thought that the Ford would certainly go unnoticed for days. He returned to the apartment, joined the others and readied himself.

The next two hours remained tense in Monica's apartment. They would leave town later that night. The group left at 1:00 a.m. in the midst of partygoers leaving clubs and bars, hoping that would make it more difficult for any police officers or FBI agents searching for them. Gargano chose an Indiana cabin as the hideout. As Daniels and the two women huddled near Gargano, he explained to them that over ten years ago, in 1956, he had spent some time in this Indiana cabin after he fled from a previous bank robbery.

Gargano shared with them that he did time in Marion for a 1956 robbery he'd committed in Franceville, Indiana. Gargano and some buddies dressed up as musical comedy farmers and robbed a bank in Franceville, about forty miles away. Gargano hid in his grandfather's cottage. They got away with $27,000 in cash. Gargano mentioned the thrill of that robbery as he grimaced in pain.

Minutes before 1:00 a.m. on Sunday, October 29, 1967, Gargano walked gingerly down the stairs out of Monica's apartment with her, Daniels and his sister Annette. Annette handed the keys to her rented 1967 white Plymouth to Daniels as she and Monica helped Gargano into the vehicle. Daniels headed toward Lake Shore Drive and eventually onto Interstate 94, which had been built a little more than ten years prior. Daniels and Annette alternated driving, switching a few times along the way. They eventually drove the car south out of Chicago, then out of Cook County and finally out of Illinois, the state that was charging them with the killing of two police officers.

Sightings

To catch a fugitive is no easy task. To catch fugitives with skills in hiding is that much more difficult. The FBI, local policemen and Cook County sheriff's deputies joined efforts as they canvassed the area in hopes of finding the robbers as they investigated and discovered who the perpetrators were for the Northlake Bank robbery. The initial thought was that they might still be in Northlake, or at least in the nearby vicinity. Police feared the bandits were holding a nearby family hostage in hopes of remaining out of sight as they planned their escape.

They knew one of the gunmen suffered from a gunshot wound. Given the amount of blood on the pavement outside the Northlake Bank and the blood smeared on the car, the gang probably sought some kind of medical attention. The wounded man, likely Henry Gargano, simply could not last that long. They swiftly notified all area hospitals of the possibility that a man with a shoulder wound might seek medical care. They gave details of their faces and body types as police stood guard at all the hospitals. Nearby Elmhurst Hospital was an option; so was Gottlieb Hospital in Melrose Park. Westlake Hospital in Melrose Park was also a possibility. Local police forces assisted one another when needed—just like this weekend.

Other areas where the fugitives might be hiding out were forest preserves. There were several in the area—they usually ran alongside a river. Policemen checked there frequently—heading back there several times to assure themselves the fugitives were not hiding in the wooded areas. The most common and the most effective means of canvassing an area was old-fashioned police work. They simply went door to door, thinking the men must have had some help. A female accomplice waiting in a parked getaway vehicle two blocks west near the Scholle Corporation was proof. And perhaps they received help in the nearby neighborhoods. Hiding in a nearby home, they likely were waiting for the police investigation to calm down—that was probably a good strategy.

Northlake police came up empty as they received tips that simply frustrated them. The fugitives were "sighted" multiple times in unlikely places, such as taverns, restaurants and stores. Unfortunately, any credible reports proved unfruitful. They were simply gone—vanished from the surrounding areas.

The only credible reported sighting that took place was in the city of Chicago, near Fullerton Avenue and Kedzie Avenue in the Logan Square area. A taxi driver in his Checker Taxi Company cab in the hours before sunrise on Monday morning claimed to have seen both Daniels and Gargano. He'd kept his eyes peeled ever since the nationwide alert was issued—he was surprised that he saw these two men in a "1962 or 1963 Buick."[126] The taxi driver did notice something odd, though. The car had Michigan license plates: NA 1806 to be exact. He reached for a pen and paper and jotted down the license plate numbers. He followed the Buick for about a mile, until it headed east on Fullerton Avenue, away from him and toward the lake. The police canvassed this northwest section of Chicago, but local authorities came up empty. The more time went on, the less hope they felt of finding the bandits. However, if this sighting was credible and accurate, then their hopes of capturing them were raised since they were still in the Chicago area. At least for now, police thought.

Putting the Pieces Together

As Chief Gilliam pieced together the crime scene, he reviewed in his mind the events that led up to the Northlake Bank robbery—the warning, that phone call they received. That's what stuck out in his mind. He willingly shared information as he disclosed that the Northlake Police Department had received a tip a few weeks before the robbery—three weeks to be exact.

On October 6, 1967, exactly three weeks prior to the robbery, a call came in to the Northlake Police Department. A woman called and told them there was going to be a bank holdup. The woman said it was just a warning. She told them to do something about it. Her warning was no empty threat, she said. She then hung up the phone.

Chief Gilliam took the warning seriously and put the Northlake Bank on high alert. Patrolmen made extra rotations to the bank and checked everything twice. They verified that nothing strange occurred in or near the bank. More than two weeks after the call was made, Northlake police decided to lift the extra surveillance order from the Northlake Bank. The warning on October 6 was likely just an empty threat. Nothing had happened, and there were no visible signs that something was about to transpire. Now, Chief Gilliam and the other investigators thought about that call. Perhaps the woman who was reportedly seen in the escape vehicle was the same woman who'd placed that call three weeks earlier. She obviously knew the gang had planned some type of robbery attempt at the Northlake Bank.

On Saturday afternoon, the FBI's investigation continued. The bandits had left two critical clues that were uncovered late Friday night. The fugitives left one clue on a bank counter and a second on the abandoned getaway car. As the FBI took meticulous steps to interview eyewitnesses in the surrounding area, they uncovered the palm prints and fingerprints on a bank counter. They took proper steps to cautiously copy these prints and send them to the lab for tracing. The second essential clue rested on the exterior of the getaway car. Those prints matched Gargano and Daniels. In addition to the blood analysis left at the bank and at the getaway car from Gargano's bleeding shoulder, the FBI now had fingerprints that matched the crime to its perpetrators. Evidence confirmed Henry Gargano and Clifton Daniels as Ronald Dale Raine's accomplices.[127]

A Cottage on the Lake

Summer is a time to get away and enjoy cool lake breezes for many Chicago residents. A popular place among Chicagoans was Fish Lake, Indiana, in Lincoln Township, exactly where Route 4 passes between Upper Fish Lake and Lower Fish Lake. About two hours away, many Chicago residents gathered there during summertime and built lasting friendships while getting away from big-city life. The Fish Lake community had about seven hundred residents, with many cottages on the lake and several bigger, nicer homes. Many of the dirt roads that led to this community had shacks and beat-up cabins, as they hosted frequent summer weekend visitors. The place was primarily known as a fishing location.

Before sunrise, Gargano and the others arrived at the cottages and quietly entered his grandfather's lakeside home in the pre-dawn darkness. Gargano clutched his right arm as he felt the throbbing pain from the gunshot wound he'd received almost two days before. He told Daniels how to quietly break into the cottage. The cottage was not a luxurious place, having poor accommodations and even poorer insulation. It was primarily a summer cottage, and with summer now gone, the gang quickly reached for blankets to find warmth.

All four of them entered, not knowing that across the way an old man was living in his cottage year round, one of the few residents who actually braved the cool winter temperatures. He had trouble sleeping that night. He awoke early on Sunday morning and, peeking through the curtains of his cabin, he noticed the strange car parked at his neighbor's cottage. Over the course of the next couple days, strange persons entered and left the cottage. "Funny," he thought, "perhaps somebody has bought this place across the road."[128]

To avoid detection, Henry Gargano and Clifton Daniels stayed in the cottage, maintaining a low profile. They knew reports had surfaced about their Northlake bank shootout on Friday morning. Media outlets picked up the story rather swiftly. With the FBI's nationwide alert, newspapers, television programs and radio outlets kept their eyes on the case. False sightings happened frequently throughout the Chicago area and around the Midwest. Newspaper headlines mentioned the Northlake Bank robbery and the death of the two Northlake cops. Northlake and the surrounding community mourned the two dead Northlake policemen—it respected and loved both of them.

On Sunday afternoon, several hours after their arrival, the crime gang decided they needed food. After all, this nearly abandoned cottage had few amenities and no food. Annette looked around the cottage and saw some tables and chairs but nothing more. There were two dirty tables and an empty refrigerator in the kitchen. The dining room had two brown-stained dining tables and two portable gasoline stoves. Besides the two lanterns, the mattress in the bedroom where her brother Gargano lay wounded and the dresser in the bedroom, this cottage offered nothing more. She thought about her brother Henry, though. He was running a high fever, and his arm wasn't getting any better. She thought the arm was infected.

Annette and Monica decided only they could leave the cottage. They needed gasoline and food to survive. So the two women told Daniels they were headed out for a few minutes to grab some much-needed amenities. The month of November was right around the corner, and that meant colder temperatures. If Daniels and Gargano intended to stay here longer, they would need gasoline to survive and plenty of nonperishable canned goods. Annette grabbed her purse and walked out of the cottage with Monica just a few steps behind her. They drove away from the cottage on the dirt road and onto Route 4. Both ladies grabbed cigarettes and smoked as their nerves settled slightly.

The local grocery store did not offer much. It wasn't one of those big fancy supermarkets they were used to in Chicago. This store was a small, local joint—but that was all they needed. They weren't looking for fancy goods. All they wanted was enough food to survive. Annette and Monica grabbed plenty of canned goods and were courteous to the locals. The locals didn't suspect them of being with the two Northlake slayers. The two women learned about each other. Annette asked questions about Monica, her brother's girlfriend. Henry had dated some interesting women in his past, she thought.

After they left the grocery store, they stopped at a nearby gasoline service station. Annette pulled the car up to the station, got out and filled the tank. As she pumped gasoline into her car, she remembered the cottage's lanterns and stoves. She then filled up a container of gasoline and hoped that would be enough for a few days. A gas station attendant, Mark Emerick, approached them and gently asked them if he could pump the gasoline for them. Annette replied they would only be there a minute. She would do it herself.

Mark remarked that if they needed anything he would be inside the service station. As he walked by the car, he noticed the bleached-blond woman sitting in the car. In the backseat of the car were several grocery bags that were presumably filled with food items. Actually, there were a lot of grocery bags, he thought, many more than for just two women.

Annette finished pumping the gas, paid for it and returned to the vehicle. The two women then sped away from the gasoline station and headed toward the cottage.

A Carpenter from Chicago

Across the road from the cottage where Gargano and the others stayed lived a man and his wife from Chicago. He was Henry Borgen, a seventy-two-year-old carpenter who resided there year round. He and his wife had moved there eleven years ago, after he retired as a carpenter. He knew the Fish Lake residents very well. Things were a little more complicated during the summers, when visitors and friends came for the great fishing in the lake, but after Labor Day weekend, the primary residents were a few owners who weathered the cold winters in the cottages. The large stockpiles of lumber to warm their homes disclosed the permanent residents. Otherwise, the homes were usually closed down by fall, with boats and fishing gear stored away. Usually no vehicles were left on the property—except the broken-down car in the driveway at Adolph Rinck's cottage.

That closed-up cottage across the way suddenly had life. The place was overgrown with weeds and grass, a clear sign no one had been around for a while. Now a newer, white car was there. A Plymouth, he realized. Borgen peeked out the window and noticed that the white car that had left in the afternoon had returned. Borgen precipitously walked over to introduce himself and to see if the owner was around.

As he approached the two women, they were unloading some groceries. The blond-haired woman was near the car while the brunette walked inside the cottage.[129]

Borgen stated he was surprised to see visitors at the cottage. He inquired of the blond-haired woman about the cottage as he quickly noticed the woman's uneasiness.

"Wait a minute," replied Monica, the blonde, as she walked quickly to the door with a bag of groceries. Annette, the brunette, walked toward Borgen.[130]

"What's going on?" the neighbor asked.[131] Annette, familiar with her grandfather's cottage, replied that the "old man was coming back to the place and they are just here to clean it up for him."[132]

Borgen thought that comment was odd. As he said goodbye to her, he sensed there were other people in the cottage. The blond woman nervously directed her attention to another person in the cottage as she unpacked the groceries. Borgen walked back home and thought to himself, "That's funny. That old man is eighty-four years old, and he moved away a year and a half ago because he's sick. I'm surprised that he's well enough to come back."[133]

As he returned to his cottage, Borgen took one last glance back and realized something suspicious was going on over there.

As soon as Borgen walked away, Annette swiftly walked into the cottage and made eye contact with Monica. They both thought that had been a close call. Annette walked into Henry's bedroom and saw him propped up on two mattresses, with part of the mattresses hanging over the small box of springs underneath. She shared with him that the neighbor had come over and talked with them as they unloaded the groceries. She told the neighbor they were there to clean up the place so the old man could come back to a clean cottage.

Henry, losing strength, said they should keep an eye on him. If the neighbor suspiciously left the cottage in his car, they were to follow him up the road, at least tail him for a bit. If need be, they would have to persuade him to refrain from calling the cops. They needed to cover their tracks.

Annette looked around the room. There wasn't much there—the dresser, two end tables, the gas lanterns and, of course, the loot that remained hidden underneath Henry's bed. Things were messy around here, that's for sure. Her brother was getting worse. He was running a higher fever than normal. And he didn't have his usual vigor. Understandable, given the circumstances, but how much longer he could last in these conditions, she simply didn't know. Medical attention was out of the question. Too many people knew too much. Newspapers, radio stations and television programs all covered the story as they traced the bandits' moves and traced law enforcement's steps to capture them. The cat and mouse game continued.

Chapter 4

OCTOBER 30–31, 1967

THE CAPTURE

Still shocked by the events that had unfolded the Friday before, the Northlake community and people all over the Midwest worked together. Residents talked to one another as they conjured future preventative measures. They shared information and discussed how something like this could have been prevented. However, as neighbors conversed with one another, there was a sense of caution in the air. The bandits were still not apprehended—danger lurked. "Police said they suspect that the fugitives are still hiding in the Chicago area and are becoming desperate for medical attention."[134] Police concentrated their efforts in the Northlake area as they distributed photos of Gargano and Daniels.

Friends visited the Perris and the Nagles, stupefied by the deaths of Anthony Perri and John Nagle. As Northlake residents tried to make sense of the robbery, Northlake police and the FBI took all necessary steps to corner Gargano and Daniels. Their investigation persisted. Immediately after learning the identity of the two remaining culprits on Saturday, police searched the Bolingbrook home of Anthony Gargano, father of Henry Gargano. They found no clues that Henry Gargano had been there anytime after the shooting.

Police put pressure on the fugitive's relatives. Anthony Gargano woke up early Monday morning still perplexed at what had occurred. He was surprised that his sons turned out this way. He had thought they would straighten out. Years ago they had moved to Bolingbrook from Chicago in hopes of improving their lives. Anthony finally found steady work at a nearby industrial plant in Lemont, just a short ride from their home, as a night watchman. He enjoyed having Annette's kids living with them in Bolingbrook. At least she did not turn out like her brothers, he thought, but Annette's kids were young and made too much noise at home for Henry. Anthony Gargano later stated that "quibbling and fighting" developed between Henry and Annette's kids. Henry had returned to live with them after his parole earlier that year. Annette, however, was put in a difficult position since she cherished her relationship with her brother.

Anthony Gargano went through questioning and pain. His other son, Michael Salvatore Gargano, was serving time in prison for murder. Michael was charged and convicted of killing a drug dealer—a peddler, as people referred to him. The stress mounted on Anthony over the years. Two sons, two murderers. Michael was sentenced to 100 to 150 years in a federal penitentiary. Michael was the leader of a crime syndicate, or so the media reported—a ruthless murderer. It was a scary thought. Anthony hoped for change after he moved to Bolingbrook. You can move out of Chicago, but the Chicago friends remain with you. They certainly remained with his sons.

As he stepped up to the podium at the Bolingbrook police station, Anthony Gargano refocused his attention. He spoke with a downcast mood and trembling voice as he pleaded to his son, "Turn yourself in, Henry."[135] "Son, give yourself up!"[136] Anthony pleaded with Henry and his partner, Clifton, in hopes they would realize their efforts to avoid law enforcement were futile. Anthony Gargano "hoped that both his son and Clifton Daniels, the other hunted gunman, would surrender before they were killed or killed others."[137] The short, white-haired man stated as he stepped away from the microphone that no more policemen needed to die. Anthony Gargano thought about the stress he'd been under over the weekend. This tension was simply too much for any person.

Reporters quickly bombarded Anthony Gargano with questions.

One reporter asked him where he thought his son was hiding.

Another reporter questioned if the younger Gargano was involved with the same crime gang as his brother.

And yet another reporter inquired about Anthony Gargano's thoughts concerning his son's innocence.

Anthony Gargano stopped and turned to reporters. "I've been through hell. I am so worried I am ready to drop dead. I urge Henry to turn himself in whether or not he actually did what they say he did."[138] Anthony later explained to reporters that he wasn't totally convinced Henry had committed the crime. Henry had done some bad things in the past, but nothing like this, he thought. Anthony told reporters one last time, "I am hoping he will get the message and that he will sit down and give it a lot of thought and consideration."[139] This was going too far, even for one of his sons.

MEANWHILE, OVER TWO HUNDRED miles south of Northlake, Illinois, there was another family willing to make an announcement. News had reached downstate Illinois that the other man being sought was Clifton Orneal Daniels from Cisne, a small rural town two hours from St. Louis. Daniels's family members were shocked by the news. Clifton had been in trouble with the law, but nothing like this. He usually did robberies here and there—small stuff. Machine gun weapons, though, were out of the ordinary for him.

The FBI contacted Daniels's relatives for assistance. Wilma, Daniels's sister, suggested that her husband, Tom Hunt, speak on behalf of the family. A local Chicago radio station, WCFL, said they wanted to put him on the air. After all, they were a growing station playing top 40 music. Their growing audience targeted twenty- to thirty-year-olds, Gargano's and Daniels's age range. Tom Hunt agreed to make an announcement, and on Monday, October 30, he made this plea: "Clifton, if you are listening to me, this is Tom. Please don't cause any more trouble. You give yourself up. If you will, you won't be hurt, and your family will feel much better about it."[140]

Tom continued, "Your family loves you, Clift. We're very sorry about this. But please, please Clift, please give yourself up, because you haven't got a chance."[141]

Tom paused for a second and then urged him again, "Wilma is sitting beside me. We both feel like this is the best thing for you to do. So, think it over, Clift. Please give yourself up, okay?"[142] As Tom stopped speaking, the DJ quickly thanked him over the air, reiterating that the best thing for them to do was to turn themselves in to authorities. Then the DJ quickly announced the next song, a top 40 music hit.

Sometimes pleadings worked; sometimes they didn't work. Sometimes criminals realized the desperate situation they were in and turned themselves in, knowing there was nothing else they could do. The Gargano and Daniels families certainly hoped that was the case now. But after such grisly events, hope seemed far off.

THE LAST ENCOUNTER between Henry Borgen and the inhabitants of Adolph Rinck's cottage came on Tuesday afternoon. On October 31, 1967, Borgen had a doctor's appointment, a regularly scheduled checkup. Borgan, who had trouble sleeping, shared with his wife that he noticed the car had been moved during the night hours. Perhaps the ladies decided to enjoy the nightlife in nearby LaPorte, he shared with his wife. But nothing threatening appeared to him. At least, not until he left for his doctor's appointment Tuesday afternoon.

As he entered his car, he wondered if Rinck's houseguests were still there, doing some "cleaning" before the eighty-four-year-old man returned to his cottage. Borgen slowly drove out of the driveway, passing the dirt road that led to Rinck's cottage. He drove toward Highway 4. Borgen then looked in his rearview mirror and noticed that the white Plymouth had pulled out of the dirt road and was following him. Borgen thought it was strange that the car was driven by the two ladies at Rinck's cottage. As soon as he turned onto Route 4, the white Plymouth stopped and returned to the dirt road. For a moment Borgen's heart raced just a little faster. He pulled out a cigarette, lit it and headed to his doctor's appointment.

Borgen thought about the two ladies at the cottage and wondered why they'd followed him. They obviously were up to no good. He thought to himself that too many things were suspicious. And if they were up to no good, they probably thought he was headed to the police station to inform police about their presence at Rinck's cottage. The irony struck him. The watcher became the watched. Later, he peeked through his curtains and looked at the strange car—a white car with Illinois license plates. They obviously were keeping an eye out for him and would immediately follow him when he pulled his car out of the driveway. The tables turned as the cottage's residents felt threatened by his presence. An old retired man with no guns was making two high-profiled bandits and two of their accomplices a little nervous.

The Investigation Continues

In Chicago's western suburbs, local police's canvassing efforts continued. In O'Hare Airport's parking lot, they found yet another clue. Police extended their investigative efforts to the airport's vicinity since reports had surfaced of a mask found on Irving Park Road. Aside from possibly escaping via car there were other means of travel, including rail and plane. Although police excluded these two travel possibilities since Gargano was wounded, fake identifications and disguises likely allowed them to travel discreetly. So on Tuesday, they found a vehicle that was traced to Clifton Daniels. That clue led police to think that his car served as a getaway vehicle. The gang's strategy involved abandoning the initial stolen robbery car close to the crime site. From there, they drove a second car that allowed them to go undetected. Finding this second getaway vehicle served as confirmation that the Northlake Bank robbers planned another exit strategy.

As of Tuesday afternoon, the FBI and police had pieced together enough evidence to confirm the Northlake Bank robbery perpetrators. From their interview of Marion Penitentiary inmates, a list was compiled of likely candidates. Two names repeatedly surfaced on the list, those of Henry Gargano and Clifton Daniels. They had both been arrested for previous robberies. They had both been paroled from prison at the beginning of the year. The second strong clue was the blood found at the Northlake Bank scene. The blood found there matched the blood in the parked getaway car at Scholle Chemical Factory. That blood matched Henry Gargano's blood type. And if Gargano was involved, then Daniels was likely his accomplice. In addition to the blood match, the finger and palm prints taken from a bank counter and on the abandoned getaway car matched those of Gargano and Daniels. The final firm evidence was Ralph Garduno's arrest. Garduno had served time with Gargano. Although he was caught alone, Garduno was the driver of a getaway car. Garduno's interrogation revealed his accomplices. That was the third major investigative discovery that confirmed the identity of the remaining two fugitives. Evidence was critical to obtain search warrants. And with search warrants came more answers to a supposed robbery crime gang.

Perri's Funeral

The Northlake Police Department worked the case locally. It canvassed and accepted all telephone leads, no matter how far-fetched they seemed. The police department had lost two fine members of its force. Emotions ran high over the weekend. However, the two victims' spouses and family members displayed even greater emotions. On Saturday, October 28, at 5:00 p.m., the events began at the Frank Granata Funeral Home at 1857 North Harlem Avenue, a few blocks north of North Avenue. That section had grown with former residents from Chicago's Little Italy, near Taylor Street. Most of the Italians who lived near Taylor Street had moved westward after plans were made to build the University of Illinois at Chicago campus there in

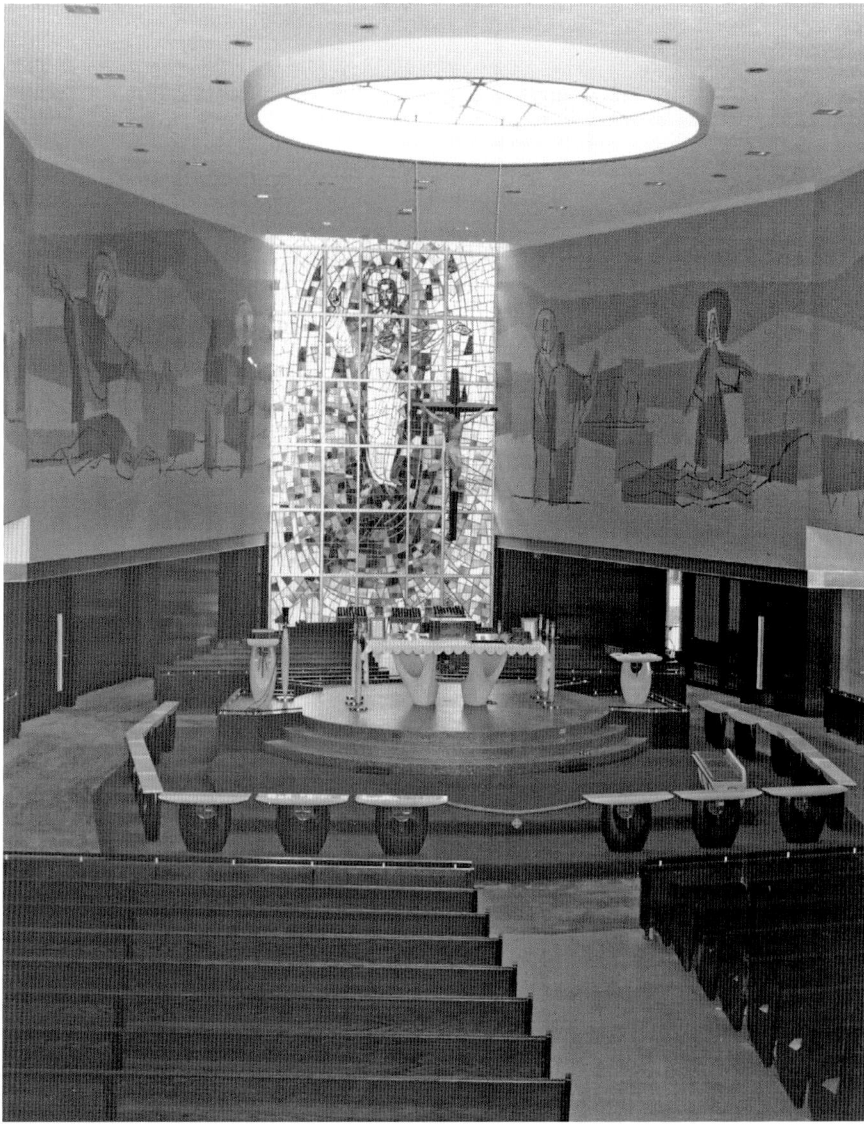

St. John Vianney Church, where Anthony Perri's funeral Mass took place with hundreds of police officers present. *Courtesy of Northlake City Hall.*

the 1960s. Neighborhoods such as the one near North and Harlem Avenues saw an influx of Italian Americans. Markets, stores and funeral homes were needed to serve the new residents. Frank Granata Funeral Home was one of the newer businesses that serviced that Italian neighborhood.

Anthony Perri's visitation was primarily for family and friends. Perri's loved ones stopped by, shared stories and mourned the horrific, senseless crime committed against him. A defenseless Perri stood no chance, many thought. Antoinette Perri cried uncontrollably, unable to stop her tears. She had lost her best friend and husband. Close family members tried to console her, but nothing worked. Sunday evening came to a close, and instructions were given for Monday, when the funeral Mass and burial were scheduled to take place.

On Monday morning, Antoinette, Ted, Ann Marie and Anthony Perri's mother, Minnie, awoke early and headed to the Frank Granata Funeral Home. Antoinette's throbbing head and mental anguish were understandable. She wore a simple black dress with a veil around her head. As she and her children sat down at the funeral home, policemen from the surrounding community filed in, signed the visitation book and saluted the copper-colored casket holding Anthony Perri, paying proper respects for the last time. Prayers were offered for Anthony Perri before the casket was closed. Antoinette cried, "My Tony! My Tony!"[143]

After they put the casket in the hearse, Antoinette and the rest of the family rode in procession in a black limousine. About seventy-five squad cars from about fifty suburbs, Cook County and the state police department formed a procession to the church.[144] Antoinette sobbed as she attempted to reconcile Anthony's death with the happy moments in their marriage. Their times growing up near Taylor Street brought some good memories back, but the pain remained and wouldn't go away. The hearse and procession continued along North Avenue as it finally reached Wolf Road in Northlake. There the hearse made a right turn as it headed for St. John Vianney Catholic Church.

St. John Vianney Catholic Church had experienced significant growth in recent years. Families that moved to Northlake created a bedroom community as workers were employed at local factories, many near O'Hare Airport. In 1952, St. John Vianney Catholic Church called a new priest to its parish, Father Edward T. Boyle. Under Father Boyle, the congregation grew and matched the community's growth. Father Boyle headed the school's establishment and its growth. Soon thereafter, a convent was added to St. John Vianney, but the biggest project came in the late 1950s, when church leaders built a new church sanctuary. The congregation sacrificed for a few years as it celebrated Mass in the basement of the church. On March 7, 1965, St. John Vianney Catholic Church dedicated its newest sanctuary.[145] The church was built in the shape of a fish with large murals that depicted events in the life of Christ. More than two years later, Father Boyle celebrated the funeral Mass for Anthony Perri.

As the hearse and procession of cars arrived at St. John Vianney, Antoinette's eyes swelled up once more. Her children unsuccessfully tried to comfort her. Northlake policemen served as pallbearers for Anthony Perri. They quickly walked to the hearse, lined up on each side of the casket and placed the casket on the trolley. Members of an honor guard from the Illinois Police Association stood outside the entrance to the church in uniform and raised their white batons as the casket was pushed through the doors. Antoinette and the others walked slowly up the aisle as they followed the casket. She and her children sat on the second pew, and she wiped tears from her eyes as she wept.

Father Boyle began the Mass with nearly five hundred attendees shedding tears. As each person listened intently, Father Boyle began his homily and made a statement about Patrolman Perri's sacrifice for the community where he lived and served.

Anthony Perri and the other policemen were "sincere, dedicated policemen" who had "gallantly rushed to the scene" of Friday's bank robbery. "If they had been a few seconds later, they might have been an entirely different story. But they gave their greatest possession—their very lives—to protect us."[146] "He loved everybody," continued Father Boyle. "When youngsters were in trouble, he talked to them like a father. In family gatherings, he liked to sing out. When man began to live in community life, he elected peers to look over him. Then there was danger, and they had to appoint someone to protect the community. Such men are those in the Northlake Police Department."[147] Father Boyle focused his attention on the policemen present as he noted their dangerous responsibilities: "You know your life is in jeopardy…if you are in a disadvantaged position you may have to offer your life."[148] He stated that God "forbids you would have to raise a weapon against another human being, but sometimes it is necessary, and then often a life is lost. This tragic incident should prompt every law enforcer to be right with God."[149] "Always be at peace with God, for you may meet up with a maniac killer or a violent, vicious criminal."[150]

Father Boyle offered some last words in prayer before he ended the funeral Mass. As the casket was led away from the altar and onto the hearse, Antoinette was no longer able to carry her anguish and yelled, "My Tony! My Tony!" She nearly collapsed and needed assistance into the limousine.

SEVERAL MILES SOUTH of St. John Vianney lie Mt. Carmel Cemetery and Queen of Heaven Cemetery in Hillside, Illinois. The Mass at St. John Vianney concluded after ninety minutes. The majority of attendants joined Antoinette and her family as they wept for Anthony Perri. The procession of seventy squad cars then drove eastward on Lake Street to Mannheim Road and then went south before turning west onto Roosevelt Road. A priest from a local parish waited for the procession.

At the interment chapel in Queen of Heaven Cemetery, Anthony Perri's cousin, Reverend Richard Ferraro of St. Charles Borromeo in Bensenville, waited for his relative to arrive. Unlike the many times they'd enjoyed together, Perri did not arrive running and ready to play. He arrived in a casket. Father Ferraro performed the requiem Mass at the chapel before a crying wife, children and mother.

At the close of the ceremony, Father Ferraro stood and spoke his last words carefully. He sprinkled the last holy water on Perri's casket. Antoinette's mind raced briefly to the many times she'd asked her husband to leave the police force. If only he had done so before Friday. The ceremony then ended with Antoinette's sobbing, "Tony! Tony! Tony!" Father Ferraro, acting as both cousin and family member, rushed to Antoinette and embraced her as she attempted to hug her husband one last time. Antoinette's pain penetrated to her innermost soul. She sighed and breathed so deeply that firemen used a "portable inhalator to revive the widow as others tried to calm" her.[151] Symbolically, the chapel's lights dimmed as the services ended for Anthony Perri, a man originally from Chicago's Little Italy neighborhood.

NAGLE'S FUNERAL

Less than a mile from St. John Vianney Church is the Northlake Funeral Home. Visitation began for the second man gunned down by the Northlake Bank robbers hours after Perri's funeral Mass. John J. Nagle's visitation began at 3:00 p.m. as friends from the Northlake police force accompanied the family. Marlene Nagle, the twenty-nine-year-old widow of John Nagle, sat quietly in the funeral home, stared at her husband's casket and realized how much he had enjoyed being a detective sergeant.

The Bellwood resident's funeral Mass took place at St. John Chrysostom Catholic Church, his family's parish. The parish's priest, Reverend Leonard Huske, addressed the four hundred people present.

"The highest praise and honor to John is in the hearts of those who knew best the kind of man he was…his life and death give us a lot to think about. Why do we die? Why do we live?"[152] Like a priest, a policeman serves others, needing to forget about himself in that service. "Those who knew John know he tried to make the choice as a policeman to give himself to others…he gave himself and became a man. John would be one of the first ones on the right side of Christ. He was kind of a wonderful example to all of us to see ourselves called by Christ to give ourselves to others. Not many of us are really called upon to give ourselves for others, but to live our daily life for others. So maybe we have a love and respect for John and wish to honor him, we will try to take to ourselves the desires and goals that he had—his desire to give himself to others."[153]

Detective Sergeant Nagle's casket was then wheeled out of the church by policemen serving as pallbearers. Chief Gilliam waited just outside the church doors and saluted his detective sergeant for the last time as his eyes welled up with tears. His thought immediately shifted to the perpetrators of this killing. They took out two of his officers and left a total of five children fatherless. Chief Gilliam took one last look as Marlene Nagle and her children walked past him. John's kids were too young for this—the oldest was only nine years of age, and the youngest was only four, probably too young to remember the details of his father's funeral.

As the hearse pulled out of the church's parking lot, eighty-five squad cars followed with their lights flashing. That was the least they could do for Northlake's detective sergeant. Detective Sergeant Nagle was then buried across the road from Anthony Perri, at Queen of Heaven Cemetery in Hillside, Illinois. Marlene cried, knowing John would never return. As attendees left the procession and dispersed, anger filled their hearts as they hoped for justice. They would receive some consolation later that day.

In the midst of mourning for their fellow policemen, Northlake police fulfilled their jobs. Ronald Dale Raine remained at Bridewell Hospital in Chicago. Chief Gilliam interrogated him over the weekend, and investigators gathered more information. They visited him several times over the weekend and on Monday in hopes that he would reveal substantial information. The name of "Randall" that Raine originally gave on Friday afternoon was simply an alias. Raine used "Jimmy" frequently as an alias too. In fact, Raine probably used several aliases during his life of crime. That seemed to be the consistent pattern—fake names to go undetected. Raine remained faithful to the personal code used by him and his accomplices: you do not share information with law enforcement about one another, especially after being captured.

Over the weekend, however, the FBI reached out to their family members in hope of gathering more information about the bandits. In addition to the urgency of contacting Gargano's and Daniels's families, they reached out to Raine's family. His mother lived in Yakima, Washington, a town several hours from Seattle. She suffered from a heart condition and was under severe stress after she learned of her son's fate on Friday. Ronald Dale Raine's mother "was under sedation."[154] They talked soon to a relative of Raine, who informed him that Ronald had had juvenile problems during high school, but nothing serious. He described Raine as "restless and unable to hold down a job."[155] Raine expressed interest in changing his life, though. He wanted to learn a trade and settle down a bit. Sadly, Raine continued to associate himself with a rough crowd who did everything but settle down.

The fugitives resided in Gargano's grandfather's cottage in northern Indiana. Gargano's condition worsened as his shoulder wound became infected. The gunshot had penetrated deep into his muscle, making it immobile. Although he attempted to gather strength, he lay motionless on his bed as he groaned from time to time. Gargano ran a high fever but refused to receive medical attention. Annette and Monica made a makeshift drain. He did not want to return to prison. Life behind bars was anything but glamorous. Receiving any kind of medical attention required disclosing his situation, and that was simply too risky.

Daniels remained in the boarded-up cottage. There wasn't much for him to do. He paced back and forth and thought about the past several months—all the robberies they'd been involved in, from Ohio to southern Illinois to Northlake. They were an established crime gang that made cops fear them. Gargano was the unquestionable leader of the group, a man Daniels had met at Marion Penitentiary. He thought about the interesting persons you meet in prison. They put a bunch of criminals together in a room, he thought. They shared stories, skills and adventures, fed off one another. Marion was a federal penitentiary, but it was also a place where criminals came together and shared ideas. It was also a place where friendships were forged, and a place where gangs came together, just like this one.

Daniels peeked one last time into Gargano's room and realized the situation was getting worse. He took a puff from his cigarette and pondered the situation. Annette and Monica had gone out a few times. They'd left again today, Monday, to get more food and to get a break from the small cottage. The old man across the street probably kept an eye on them, he thought. That wasn't a good thing. Time was of the essence, but nothing could be done. He was torn between escaping on his own and remaining with Gargano. They'd worked together on too many jobs the past few months. Either they were going to get caught or they were going to wait until Gargano's health improved or worsened until death. There wasn't much of a choice. Everything was coming to a head. As he paced around the cottage's small living room, his attention turned to Annette and Monica.

Beginnings

Gargano and Daniels talked briefly about their robberies throughout the course of the weekend. They had traveled to several places throughout the Midwest doing "jobs," as they referred to their robberies. Gargano simply shared snippets here and there—nothing concrete. Daniels chimed in, adding his own adventures as if they were folklore. However, now that their capture seemed imminent, and Gargano's life hung in the balance, Daniels shared with Annette and Monica about the group's escapades. They worked together as a team, almost as if they were running a military operation.

Daniels explained that life outside prison walls was tough. He, Gargano and Raine loved the thrill of robbing banks. They excelled at robberies. Both he and Gargano had worked for a contractor in Lyons, a Chicago suburb. Gargano worked as a sewer worker, but he eventually quit after he "got some steel in his eyes."[156] They both were fired from their jobs for absenteeism. Although they tried, they weren't accustomed to the scheduled times for work. Through some mutual friends, both of them established a friendship with Ronald Dale Raine from Washington. Raine spent plenty of time in prison, just like them. His criminal record was as long as their own records.

All three figured robbing banks was the thrill they needed. They loved high-powered weapons, and they loved the narcissistic adventures of robbing banks and supermarkets. On Thursday, July 20, 1967, Ronald Dale Raine rented an apartment in Bellwood, Illinois. It was a second-floor flat with two bedrooms, a living room area and a bathroom—nothing fancy but enough to live on their income. They found an advertisement for it in a local newspaper and contacted the person on the first floor, Marie Vazquez. She lived with her husband and child on the first floor. The owner agreed to rent them the apartment, and they secured the second-floor apartment through

November 20. That was their home base. All three men moved around from time to time, but they pretty much referred to the Bellwood apartment as home for those three months. They planned their robberies from there.

Daniels shared with both women about their string of robberies, but primarily with Annette. As their conversation continued inside the Indiana cottage, the FBI diligently worked at finding this now notorious crime gang. Local law enforcement officials canvassed the area and searched neighborhoods and possible hideouts—everything from local forest preserves to local motels along Mannheim Avenue, the road that led to O'Hare Airport. The FBI looked at the crime gang as a puzzle that needed to be put together. They interviewed Marion prisoners, family members and parole officers to obtain the best angle on their whereabouts. Unbeknownst to many persons involved in the case, the FBI found an informant who shared valuable information. She knew the gang and some of their actions, although not all of them. The FBI assured her that they would look favorably on her for any information. So she shared her knowledge. The FBI pieced together more clues to the crime puzzle. Besides the informant's knowledge, a Gargano family member mentioned a cottage in northern Indiana during questioning. She also mentioned an apartment in Bellwood, just a few miles away from the Northlake Bank. That might be their hideout, she said. The police intently listened.

The FBI was curious to know about all the property that each of their family members owned. They focused on both Gargano's and Daniels's relatives. Both men's relatives provided housing and protection. Daniels grew up in rural Illinois, while Gargano was raised in the city of Chicago. Along with his brother, Michael, Henry Gargano's extensive relationship with crime syndicates was a concern. The FBI received valuable information and focused on the family cottage hidden on an Indiana lake. They discussed whether approaching that cottage was safe and worth the risk. The high-powered weapons in the men's previous crimes posed a serious threat. If the FBI was to be successful, they had to act cautiously.

The Parks Brothers Robbery

An early heist was the Parks Brothers robbery in Plainfield, Illinois. Located on Route 59, the gang had robbed the supermarket on Sunday, July 23. The store manager, later identified as Richard Gehrke, entered the store prior to opening, about ten minutes before 7:00 a.m. The masked thieves had entered the store through a vent that was open on the roof and went undetected by any security system. The thieves surveyed the store—including items and cash registers. They had looked near the registers but didn't find any money. They waited. They thought there was likely a store safe.

As Gehrke entered the store, two men held a gun to his head. The two thieves forced Gehrke to open the store's safe, which contained about $3,000 in cash. The crooks got what they were after—money! Gehrke had remained calm, but adrenaline rushed through him. As he fumbled to open the safe, the thieves heard keys shuffling near the entrance as the store's owner, Frank Park, entered the supermarket.

Thinking their heist was at risk, the bandits immediately handcuffed both Gerhke and Parks to a meat rack. They left the premises quickly to avoid detection. The masked men took Parks's keys, removed their masks as they walked out of the store and headed toward Parks's car. Parks and Gerhke tried to escape, but they could not get out of the handcuffs, and the store's phone was out of reach. The two bandits calmly walked out of the store, started Parks's car and took off without being noticed. There were no abnormalities for any passersby. Soon thereafter, the thieves had abandoned the car near Interstate 55 in efforts to avoid police detection. After all, someone had likely walked into the store and called the authorities. The police would surely look for Parks's car. And they would find it, abandoned. The Parks Brothers robbery was one of the gang's first robberies.

The White Fence Farm Robbery

Since its opening in the 1920s, White Fence Farm had developed a loyal following. Located in Romeoville on Joliet Road, White Fence Farm was located on a major road near Interstate 55, which provided a great location for both customers and robbers. Robert Hastert, the farm's owner, had his home on the same property as the restaurant, near the back of it. Trouble began on September 4, 1967, minutes before midnight.

Typical of most workdays, the restaurant had required cleaning after closing. Hastert had assisted a few other employees, who left sooner than he did. A watchman stayed behind and kept guard during the night hours. Hastert had secured the restaurant's door behind him and walked toward his car. Along his path was a delivery truck, where several men went unnoticed. Hastert always took precautionary steps, such as having watchmen, and he felt safe. Suddenly, after he had passed the delivery truck, a few men jumped out and grabbed him, which startled him. They quickly interrogated Hastert to determine the total number of persons still inside the restaurant. Hastert told him a watchman remained during night hours but that a few employees were still inside. Just after answering them, Hastert felt a blow to his head that knocked his glasses off. Hastert briefly lost consciousness and then felt the thieves pull him into a nearby field filled with shrubbery. They all waited quietly as the remaining few employees left the premises, leaving the lone watchman for the night, typical of most workdays.

A bandit then pulled a gun, pointed it at Hastert and ordered him back to the restaurant. Hastert kept a false counter, where he usually kept a safe. Hastert, however, soon realized these bandits knew more than they should as they walked quickly toward the hidden safe. The robbers then knocked the dial off but failed to open the safe. The safe required two security keys to open it. The thieves and Hastert quietly remained in the room, unknown to the armed watchman, who had walked to the other side of the restaurant and secured the building. Hastert had willingly called the watchman in an attempt to secure his safety. Surprised to hear the owner's voice, the watchman walked into the room startled by what he saw—several gunmen holding Hastert at gunpoint. Actually, the gunmen had sawed-off shotguns, an M-1 rifle, revolvers and walkie-talkies. They were more armed than a small-town militia. The men demanded the watchman's gun. He willingly gave it to them. The gunmen then led both the watchman and Hastert to separate upstairs rooms and locked them inside. Unwilling to leave the scene, the gunmen carried the two safes they found out of the property. They were going to load the safes unto the delivery truck and open them in another location.

Suddenly, Hastert heard the gunmen moving both safes downstairs. Hastert risked capture as he opened the door to run. The thieves downstairs heard Hastert's footsteps and saw a figure run past them. One bandit did not hesitate. He fired his gun at Hastert but missed; Hastert stopped. The gunman ran to Hastert, turned his revolver around and hit Hastert over the head with the butt of his gun. Hastert decided the money in the safes paid for the worker's wages. It was worth the risk. Besides, they had earned each penny as his workers were diligent at White Fence Farm. Hastert soon recovered from the second blow to his head.

Across the field, at Hastert's home, his wife awoke to realize her husband was not yet home—he was usually home minutes past midnight. She looked at the clock on her nightstand and realized it was almost 3:00 a.m. A quick rush of adrenaline rushed through her body and jolted her out of bed and to the telephone. She dialed the restaurant's phone to reach her husband. The gunmen forced Hastert to pick up the phone and tell the person calling that everything was fine—he was simply doing last-minute cleaning. This time Hastert had been shoved inside a restaurant cooler. The bandit responsible for locking up Hastert in the cooler reached for his walkie-talkie to communicate with the sole gunman waiting outside the restaurant. After a brief discussion, the gunmen decided to expedite their robbery and used a nearby forklift to place the safes inside the delivery truck. However, that proved more difficult than anticipated, and they abandoned the plan after Hastert's wife called. The three gunmen left White Fence Farm in a 1962 car, without the safes.

Meanwhile, back home, Hastert's wife remained uneasy about her husband's late work at the restaurant. She had decided to call her son and told him Hastert had remained at the restaurant doing work three hours later than usual. Her son drove there to check out the situation. But before he left, he dialed the police and told them to do a well-being check at the restaurant. Hastert seemed normal, but working this late was simply unusual. At the same time, Hastert opened the cooler, walking slowly since he thought the gunmen remained inside. He picked up a nearby phone, dialed his wife and told her the situation. His wife said that the cops had already been called. They were on their way.

After securing the premises, the police questioned Hastert and the night watchman. Hastert described the gunmen: three males, one in his thirties and one several years younger. All three men wore masks and hats; one man wore a green military-style beret. They all had dark clothing, and they used high-powered military-style weapons and walkie-talkies. The police took the report and noted the information on their internal system. Hastert's description proved vital—gunmen went on several robberies in the coming months. They matched physical descriptions and matched their military-style weapons.

The Harrisburg Kroger Robbery

On Saturday, September 9, 1967, Gargano, Daniels and a third man robbed a Harrisburg, Illinois supermarket. The Kroger market was on a major road, U.S. Highway 45, just outside the city's town. Soon after Kroger closed at 8:00 p.m., two robbers walked into the store while a third man waited outside and looked out for police officers. The store's doors were locked, and one of the men asked to return his carton of milk. He repeatedly stated that he purchased spoiled milk and needed to make an exchange. The store manager, Harold Hastings, allowed them to enter the store. The two men made more than an exchange—they robbed the supermarket.

With revolvers in hand, both men ordered the store manager to give them the checks and money that came from that day's transactions. Hastings retrieved the money and handed it over to them. Hastings briefly made eye contact with one thief who looked familiar to him. He had quickly sifted through many of the day's customers and remembered that same customer buying the carton of milk. Perhaps the man made the initial purchase to scout the premises and count the number of employees. Since Harrisburg was a small and quiet town, security was minimal. Hastings thought that these type of crimes happened in urban areas, not in small towns—and certainly not in Harrisburg.

As Hastings broke eye contact with the thief, he quickly thought about the .45-caliber and .38-caliber guns these two men held. Only three other employees were in the store—Curtis Healy, Ken Clore and Linda Albert. Hastings hoped the bandits would take the small amount of money, depart the store and not hurt any of the employees.

The only tense moment happened when the bandits looked inside the bag and realized there was not much in there. One bandit quickly exclaimed, "Is this all?"[157] Hastings humbly responded that they'd made two deposits that day, so money was low during closing hours. Then Hastings saw a car pull up to the Kroger store.

Kroger employee Curtis Healy was usually picked up at the store. His parents, along with his sister Karen, pulled up to the store as they looked for Curtis. The third robber quickly noticed them. He commanded them out of the vehicle and into the store. Soon, there were too many people inside the Kroger store. The longer this continued, the worse the situation could become, for both the victims and the bandits. The bandits talked briefly before they ordered the whole group into the store coolers. The bandits took Hastings's keys and then ordered them not to open the cooler doors. If they opened the doors, the robbers would shoot them. Hastings ordered everyone in the coolers to remain calm. They all waited for about fifteen minutes. They were all in the cooler, petrified, when Hastings decided to open the cooler doors, hoping the bandits were gone. As he poked his head out, he didn't notice any remnants of the thieves. Besides, they had taken his car keys. All three of them were gone.

The three bandits disappeared soon after they ordered all of their victims into the coolers. They drove away in Hastings's 1959 red Plymouth. The three bandits now likely had two cars—the one they arrived in and Hastings's car. They drove south on U.S. Highway 45 before heading north on Route 34. They then decided to abandon the stolen car.

Hastings quickly called the police department to notify it of the evening's events. The police arrived, took the victims' reports and quickly drove throughout the surrounding area in an attempt to capture three bandits and Hastings's red Plymouth.

A FEW DAYS LATER, on Monday, a local resident walked along his property and noticed something strange. In the midst of cornfields, George Barnes noticed a red object that was indistinguishable from afar. As he walked closer, he realized it was a red Plymouth with no one inside the vehicle. Barnes called the police instead of meddling with the car. Local police officers matched the red Plymouth to Harold Hastings, Kroger's store manager. However, no other evidence pointed to the bandits. The police dusted the car in search of fingerprint evidence. That would take some time, though, since they had to send the prints to the laboratory for processing.

AS THE FBI'S INVESTIGATION of the Northlake Bank robbery surged ahead as local law enforcements canvassed the area, news surfaced that police in Harrisburg had finished their own research. The day prior to the October 27 Northlake Bank robbery, the employees who were temporarily held captive at the Kroger store were shown a picture of Clifton Daniels. Daniels was positively identified as one of the thieves who broke into the store. Police charged Daniels that day with the Harrisburg Kroger robbery.

Five days later, on the morning of their capture, those same employees were shown a picture of Henry Gargano. Gargano was also positively identified as one of the robbers. Later on the day he was identified as one of the three bandits, Gargano faced more serious charges. The crime gang's run of assaulting supermarkets and banks was quickly coming to an end. Instead of the high-end lifestyle they'd enjoyed for many months, they potentially faced a lifetime of less superior food quality and imprisonment.

The Canton Robbery Continued

Gargano, Daniels and Raine met up with another former prisoner in Ohio: Ralph Garduno. Garduno drove one of the getaway cars at the October 13 A&P store robbery. They had planned to calmly walk away from that robbery with no injuries. Daniels thought that robbery would be easy with their high-powered weapons and two getaway vehicles with two drivers. Their job was to walk in calmly and act like regular customers. If they went unnoticed, they would walk out like regular customers. Everything should have gone without a hitch. But then a police cruiser pulled up, and all hell broke loose. Garduno was caught soon after the robbery. Gargano had wanted him to drive a getaway car to provide additional backup in case cops showed up. Well, the cops showed up, and the shooting began. Their machine guns struck fear in police officers. All the cops used were revolvers. It was like the military against civilians with guns. Daniels thought there was no match. From there, they headed north in hopes of taking a different route to Chicago. However, a cop car followed them for some distance. They were forced to evade the police car. Gargano put his head out of the window and started shooting. Eventually, they turned onto a side road and lost the cops. After they returned to Bellwood, the thrill of committing robberies continued.

The National Guard Armory Robbery

Their next adventure occurred twenty miles from Marion Federal Penitentiary. In prison, inmates always shared stories. A few inmates talked about an armory in the nearby town of Salem. It was the National Guard Armory. On October 20, 1967, at 7:15 p.m., all three bandits executed their plan of robbing the National Guard Armory. Gargano, wearing a mask to cover his face, entered the armory while Daniels and Raine waited by another entrance. Gargano discreetly worked his way around the building when he came upon a janitor who was polishing the floors. The large buffer made a raucous noise and prevented the janitor from hearing the approaching thief. The thief pointed a revolver at the janitor and said, "We don't want to hurt you, just do as we tell you."[158] The robber pressed the gun against the back of the janitor and forced him to the front door. The armory's front doors were on the building's east side, where two additional thieves waited. They also wore masks, and they carried sawed-off shotguns.

They quickly forced the janitor to sit on a bucket in a small cleaning closet as he faced the wall. As one thief kept an eye on him, the other two masked men looked for the supply room. The janitor's temporary guardian paced back and forth and displayed a sawed-off shotgun. The two men returned and forced the janitor toward the southwest part of the building, where the supply room was located. They forced the janitor to sit on a chair just outside the supply room.

The same two robbers took the janitor's keys. The thieves unsuccessfully attempted to unlock the vault with the keys. They shot the lock with a gun and eventually broke their way into the weapons storage room. They found many useful items, including high-powered weapons. They grabbed one for each member of the group. The thieves had led the janitor to the weapons vault, forced him to sit in a steel chair and then taped his arms to prevent him from leaving. The janitor's feet were secured to each other with string—he was unable to leave and call for help. As the bandit responsible for the janitor left the room, he said there was plenty of air "through that hold down there."[159] Later that night, the police were called due to the lights that remained on in the armory for an extraordinary amount of time. The janitor was rescued and shared his fearful experience that night.

Gargano, Daniels and Raine left a little after 8:00 p.m. All three of them avoided detection. The sergeant responsible for the armory and others arrived at the armory and eventually called local police, who canvassed the armory. They found evidence of weapons stolen and a janitor tied to a steel chair in the weapons vault. An inventory was then quickly taken of the missing items:[160]

One Metascope, SN 336
Infra-red detection device
Three leather holsters, flap style for .45-caliber automatic pistol
One pair of 6x30 binoculars M-3
One case one thousand rounds, .30-caliber, linked cartridges, loaded 4-ball and 1 tracer
One or two cases, Lot WC 6730 (two thousand rounds) cartridges ball, caliber .45
Two magnetic compasses
One Galvanometer, used to measure line voltage for demolition wire connections
One technical manual, M-60 machine gun, caliber 7.62
One technical manual for Browning automatic rifle

Two cans adhesive paste, each half a pound for adhering explosives to surfaces
Fifty holder blasting cap, M165
A plastic cylinder with about a half-inch hole into which blasting cap is inserted with reduced hole for wire in the other end
One half-pint can sealing compound used to moisture-proof blasting cap connections
One two-hundred-foot coil electrical wire on a metal spool similar to doorbell wire, tan in color

What disconcerted the investigators were the missing weapons: three Browning automatic rifles, model No. 1918A2. The Browning rifles were military weapons. With a rich history, they were initially used during World War II. Production increased during the Korean War when Connecticut's Royal Typewriter Company received an order for more than sixty thousand Browning M1918A2s. These newer versions were made with Arma Steel cast receivers and trigger housings. Soldiers gained affinity for the 1918A2 rifle's light weight and portability. Those same characteristics made the crime gang's use of the Browning Automatic Rifle 1918A2 so dangerous: lightweight, portable and able to shoot five hundred rounds per minute. It was a dangerous weapon in the hands of dangerous men. Any police officer who engaged criminals with these weapons was at a great disadvantage.

These were the weapons that were used at the Northlake Bank robbery a week later. These potent weapons proved too much for the four responding policeman. The Northlake Bank robbery was the gang's culmination of robberies over several months.

As Northlake police and local law enforcement canvassed the western suburbs, the FBI diligently focused on administrative tasks. The concentrated interviews proved vital to their efforts. The FBI put together information from the various inmates who had worked with the escaped criminals. Unknown to many law enforcement officials who worked the case, an FBI agent developed a relationship with a certain former fellow inmate of Gargano. The man suggested that they had made contact several times in the past few months. Gargano bragged to him that he was dating four to five women at a single time and spent $400 to $500 a week. He funded his life outside prison walls through bank robberies. The federal parole program was nullified. He and Daniels did not work in the fields they were prepared for in prison but resorted to their previous expertise—robberies. Working at those jobs proved difficult.

They attempted to comply with the law, but those types of jobs were not what they were skilled to do.

Gargano, the stronger of the two personalities, clearly enjoyed living the higher-end lifestyle. He dated several women at a time and ate at the best restaurants Chicago offered. The information passed on to the FBI continued during the course of those days. Then, on October 31, 1967, the FBI received crucial information. At about 2:00 p.m., they learned that Gargano's maternal grandfather owned a cabin in Indiana, near Fish Lake. The person shared with them that this cabin might be a likely hideout for the fugitives. The cabin was well hidden in a semi-remote area with few residents during this time of year. The FBI special agent assigned to the case quickly notified his superiors about the tip they had received. Given the national attention the Northlake Bank bandits had received since the previous Friday, they were glad to have a concrete lead. The FBI agents did their own canvassing. They were not on the scene like the local law officials were; they simply canvassed documents, conducted interviews and interrogated penitentiary officials to learn and understand the Northlake robbers.

The Capture

2:20 p.m., October 31, 1967

FBI director Marlin Johnson quickly contacted Sheriff Clifford Arnold of the LaPorte County Sheriff's Office for assistance. The conference call consisted of Sheriff Arnold, the FBI office in South Bend and a local sergeant well acquainted with the location of Adolph Rinck's cottage. The FBI told them Gargano and Daniels would not hesitate to shoot at police officers. They had shot Canton police officers a few weeks before the Northlake shootout. The plan was to do initial surveillance to identify their location, report back to the FBI and notify other local law enforcement officials for assistance.

Soon after the conversation ended, Sheriff Arnold and FBI agent Eugene Norris drove to the cottage in an unmarked car. Their objective was simple reconnaissance: observe and gather information. They parked the unmarked car about a block away to go undetected. Aside from the abandoned car at the cottage, they noticed a white automobile. Obviously people were residing there. Sheriff Arnold and Agent Norris then returned to the LaPorte sheriff's office to report their findings: the bandits were likely hiding at the cottage. A raid to get the suspects out was their best option, but if these fugitives were as dangerous as their history indicated, the law enforcement personnel had to be strategic with enough police forces to provide backup. To avoid any fugitive escape, an FBI agent and LaPorte County officer were placed some distance away. They remained undetected and reported to home base only if they saw any member of the cottage leaving the premises.

5:00 p.m., October 31, 1967

Shortly before 5:00 p.m., FBI agents, sheriff's deputies and Indiana state troopers headed to the cottage, anticipating a firefight. They discussed the fugitive's viciousness, reiterating multiple times that the robbers had shot six police officers and aimed directly with intent to kill. In fact, a Northlake police officer was shot twelve times in the firefight. To underestimate this group was to risk your own life.

As the procession of police cars, both marked and unmarked, approached the cottage, the fugitives remained inside, oblivious to what was happening. A total of seventeen law officials surrounded the cottage. The two stoves Annette and Monica had purchased the previous Monday helped keep them warm, but the cottage's poor insulation coupled with the cool temperatures made the cottage uncomfortable. Gargano's situation did not allow for flight. Their brief respite from the cold occurred on Monday night when they huddled in the car to keep warm. Aside from that, those days in the cottage were cold. All four of them were trying to stay warm inside when suddenly they heard a bullhorn.

FBI agent Norris pulled the bullhorn to his mouth and shouted, "This is the FBI, state and county police! The house is completely surrounded. All occupants immediately come out of the front door with their hands up."[161] All the local law enforcement officials present had their guns ready to fire. They were prepared for whatever heroics any of the fugitives attempted. There was no response from the cottage's residents after the bullhorn announcement.

Meanwhile, inside the cottage, Annette, Monica and Daniels quickly gathered. Daniels told them they should just turn themselves in to the authorities. The authorities just wanted him and Gargano. They were part of the larger network of robbers that had hit supermarkets and banks alike for months now. Their run had come to an end. Gargano lay on the two mattresses, slumped over as he mustered energy, and told them to place the Smith and Wesson .357 Magnum revolver under the mattress. They complied with his demand. The gun was cocked, ready to be fired. Gargano mentioned that if the FBI was involved, they should surrender. Their journey had come to an end. Annette and Monica then walked to the kitchen, where those outside the cottage saw them.

FBI Agent Norris pulled the bullhorn to his mouth once more, pressed the button and shouted again, "This is the FBI, state and county police! The house is completely surrounded. All occupants immediately come out of the front door with their hands up."[162] The two women shuffled their feet back and forth in the kitchen, as if to say that they were surrendering. Both Annette and Monica raised their arms and walked through the doors backward. Indiana and county police rushed to them, handcuffed them and ushered them into the police squad car. Both women gave no resistance. Their task was accomplished. No shots were taken in the initial phase of the arrests.

FBI agent Norris raised the bullhorn for the third time and commanded Daniels and Gargano to surrender. Their criminal run had ended. Daniels made sure everything was in place in Gargano's room. Gargano wanted the cocked gun to remain there, loaded. Daniels then walked away from the room. The only light emanating from the cottage was the kerosene lamp the two woman had purchased on Sunday. The kerosene lamp flickered because of its low level of fuel, symbolically suggesting the Northlake Bank robbers' end. Daniels paced to the kitchen and made himself noticeable to the authorities. Daniels turned the door's knob, raised his hands high in the air and walked out backward. He then said, "Don't shoot. I'm not armed, and I don't want trouble!"[163] Daniels took several steps onto the front lawn before police officers approached and tackled him. They handcuffed him and placed him in the squad car. Now Annette, Monica and Daniels were placed in separate police cars.

The tension continued for a short while longer as Gargano, the remaining fugitive, remained inside. Previous reports had made it clear that Gargano had a mean streak. Authorities knew of his hatred for any kind of authority, particularly law enforcement. The FBI agent, for the final time, demanded that he come out peacefully with his hands raised. They were going to take any act of aggression seriously. The cottage was completely surrounded, so thoughts of escape were simply dreams.

Suddenly, Annette became agitated and started yelling as she sat inside the squad car. She screamed at the police officers. Unable to ignore her, police officers walked up to her and told her to be quiet. She explained in an agitated manner that Gargano was badly hurt and lying in bed. She told them he was unable to move. The sheriff, along with the FBI agent, then walked into the cottage slowly, anticipating some form of resistance. Agent Norris commanded Gargano to remain still. As they cautiously walked through the door, they noticed a body on the two mattresses. The darkened room provided yet another dangerous obstacle. As they walked cautiously into the room, they recognized it was Gargano.

Gargano stated, "I do not have a gun."[164] Both officials then placed handcuffs on him as they noticed the makeshift drain on his right arm. They proceeded to read him his Miranda rights. Gargano told both men there was a Magnum revolver underneath the mattress, near his left foot. Agent Norris then reached underneath the mattress, grabbed the gun and noticed that it was cocked in position, ready to be fired. Gargano then uttered that if he could have reached for the gun, he would have blown the agent's brains out.

Agent Norris asked if other weapons were present. Gargano replied in a low tone that there was another gun in the adjoining bed. Norris searched the bed and found a .45 Colt automatic. The Colt had a clip with seven cartridges, with one cartridge ready in the chamber. That gun was ready to be fired, too. Gargano's right arm was immobile and had sanitary napkins with an attached rubber hose that functioned as a tourniquet. Agent Norris demanded to know if there were any other weapons. Gargano stated clearly, "We didn't use any. This is all we had."[165]

A few of the other agents proceeded inside the cottage and looked around for evidence. They wanted to know the money's whereabouts. Gargano told them the location of the zippered suitcase and a sack that contained some money. Gargano then clearly told them, "That's all the money we got."[166] The cops retrieved $39,637.00 bearing Northlake Bank wrappers; $32,732.00 was found in the blue nylon zippered bag, $5,000.00 was wrapped by a rubber band and $1,905.00 was contained in a paper bag.[167] Daniels carried $1,270.12 of his personal money on his person.[168] The rest of their belongings were sorted out later. Much of the money was missing.

Since Gargano was weak from the gunshot, the sheriff called an ambulance. As they waited for the ambulance, the authorities told him he was welcome to make a statement. Gargano initially refused to make any statements. As he was wheeled into the ambulance, he spoke briefly. "If I wasn't so weak I would have killed the first guy to come through the door and then killed myself."[169] The ambulance took him to the local hospital.

Gargano remained under heavy guard, a situation similar to the one his fellow crime partner Ronald Dale Raine had found himself in the previous Friday.

Daniels, Annette and Monica were taken to the LaPorte County Jail, where they were held overnight. Sheriff Arnold's wife, Opal Arnold, served as the jail matron. She was primarily responsible for both women. The preceding week's events stunned her. She could not understand why men engaged police in such a vicious manner. Life there was different from big-city Chicago. Throughout the time of their stay, both women laughed and maintained jovial spirits, as if their adventure had brought them exhilaration and, now, relief.

Monica gave a statement to police. She described to them the events from Annette, Daniels and Gargano's arrival. She denied involvement in the planning and execution of the Northlake Bank robbery. She merely provided assistance once she saw Gargano's situation. She hoped her cooperation would provide leniency.

Annette declined to comment. Her decision was to seek legal counsel first and then take appropriate steps from there. Her demeanor did not differ from Monica's. They both laughed when asked about the remaining Northlake Bank money. Both women awaited a federal hearing the following morning, Wednesday.

Clifton Daniels's attitude was different than the women's. Daniels was remorseful for his actions. After giving his signed statement to police, Daniels was interrogated once more. Like Monica Conner, he hoped for leniency. Unlike Monica Conner, he was a main participant in the robbery. Daniels's head slumped downward as he sobbed repeatedly. He quickly said, "I'm sorry I did this."[170] Daniels was immediately led back to his cell, where he awaited a federal hearing for charges of bank robbery the following morning. After their hearing, all three of them were returned to Chicago.

Four miles south of the crime gang's robbery in Northlake, another search began. The unknown informant provided critical information to the FBI: the Bellwood hideout.[171] As FBI agents and police officers approached the Bellwood home on the 600 block of South Twenty-fourth Avenue, they realized the proximity to Detective Nagle's Bellwood home. As Nagle's family received news that Nagle was shot to death, the Northlake Bank robbers circuitously proceeded to their own Bellwood second-floor apartment. Gargano bled profusely—that was evident from the crime scene at the bank and from the abandoned getaway vehicle at Scholle Chemical Factory.

The two-story wood house had a dilapidated garage in the back. Inside that garage was the first clue: the 1966 Chevrolet the bandits used as their second getaway vehicle. The FBI agents peeked inside the car and noticed a bloodstained cloth on the front seat. That was likely the cloth Gargano used to apply pressure on his right arm as he slumped over on the trip from the Scholle Chemical Corporation to this location. On the passenger side lay a high-powered rifle. The rear seats had "two overcoats drenched in blood, a straw hat, an overnight bag, and a weapon underneath the back seat."[172] The FBI agents definitely found valuable evidence here, but as they entered the second-floor apartment, they came across a gold mine of evidence and information that eventually allowed them to learn more about the Northlake Bank robbers.

One of the apartment's two bedrooms had a bloodstained mattress. Shotguns, rifles and handguns lined the walls just beneath the opened windows. Police quickly drew the conclusion that the two fugitives, Daniels and Gargano, had awaited approaching authorities with yet another firefight on their minds. Both men possessed a large cache of weapons to maintain their ground. As the authorities searched the apartment for more evidence, they came across more bloody rags and bloody bandages. Their search continued during the course of the night as they quickly drew neighbors' attention and provided a grisly scene for the costumed children trick-or-treating that Halloween night. In many ways, the scariest house that night was the former Bellwood home of Ronald Dale Raine, Henry Gargano and Clifton Daniels—a macabre scene indeed.

As FBI agents collected evidence, they were astonished at the amount of weapons stored in the apartment. Marie Vazquez, the first-floor resident, was perplexed by the number of FBI agents and police officers present. Police officers quickly descended on the house and closed off sections to any passing vehicles. They talked to the Vazquez family and asked them to refrain from speaking to any media outlets. Without hesitation, the family agreed to remain quiet. The presence of so many law enforcement officials startled them.

The FBI gathered the evidence prior to placing it in a van for processing. The weapons found were:[173]

One .38 revolver
Two .45-caliber machine guns
Multiple .45-caliber gun clips taped together
One 12-gauge shotgun
One telescope

Two tripods
Three .30-caliber Browning Automatic Rifles
Multiple cartridge adapter rings
Multiple cases of .30-caliber ammunition

There were enough weapons and enough firepower to supply a small militia. Police officers' chances of survival against these bandits were small.

10:00 a.m., November 1, 1967

Daniels was led from the jail to the La Porte County Courthouse across the street, handcuffed to a United States marshal. U.S. commissioner Roger Gay proceeded with the charges. Daniels whispered to confirm he understood the charges as he hung his head in an act of submission. Commissioner Gay then asked Daniels if he would like a lawyer. Daniels replied, "No."[174] Daniels was charged with federal crimes of bank robbery and crossing state lines to avoid prosecution. The arrest warrants that provided for Daniels's and Gargano's arrests included the killing of two policemen. Initial thoughts were that they would be eligible for the death penalty for the federal crime of murder during a bank robbery.

Annette and Monica were both charged with being accessories to the crimes of bank robbery and harboring criminals. Annette asked for a court-appointed lawyer. She simply did not have the funds to pay for an attorney. Monica claimed unemployment since she had surely lost her job.

Unlike the others, Gargano did not have a hearing. Gargano was under sedation from the gunshot wound to his arm, so no hearing was held for him. Gargano underwent surgery and was not in the proper state of mind to have charges read to him. That would occur at another time. However, Anthony Gargano and his wife did make the trip to La Porte, Indiana, to support their son and daughter, now accessories to bank robbery. The Garganos walked into the county jail with their heads hung low, saddened by the tragic events that had unfolded the previous week.

November 3, 1967

Dr. Howard did not see the blond-haired woman again in person. The only contact between them came several days later, on Thursday. At around noon that day, Dr. Howard was sitting in his office when he received a telephone call. A man on the other end threatened the doctor and told him that he was Miss Conner's relative. The caller told Dr. Howard, "She's in enough trouble now. You better keep your mouth shut."[175] The caller then ended the phone call. He never gave his name, and he never called again. Dr. Howard

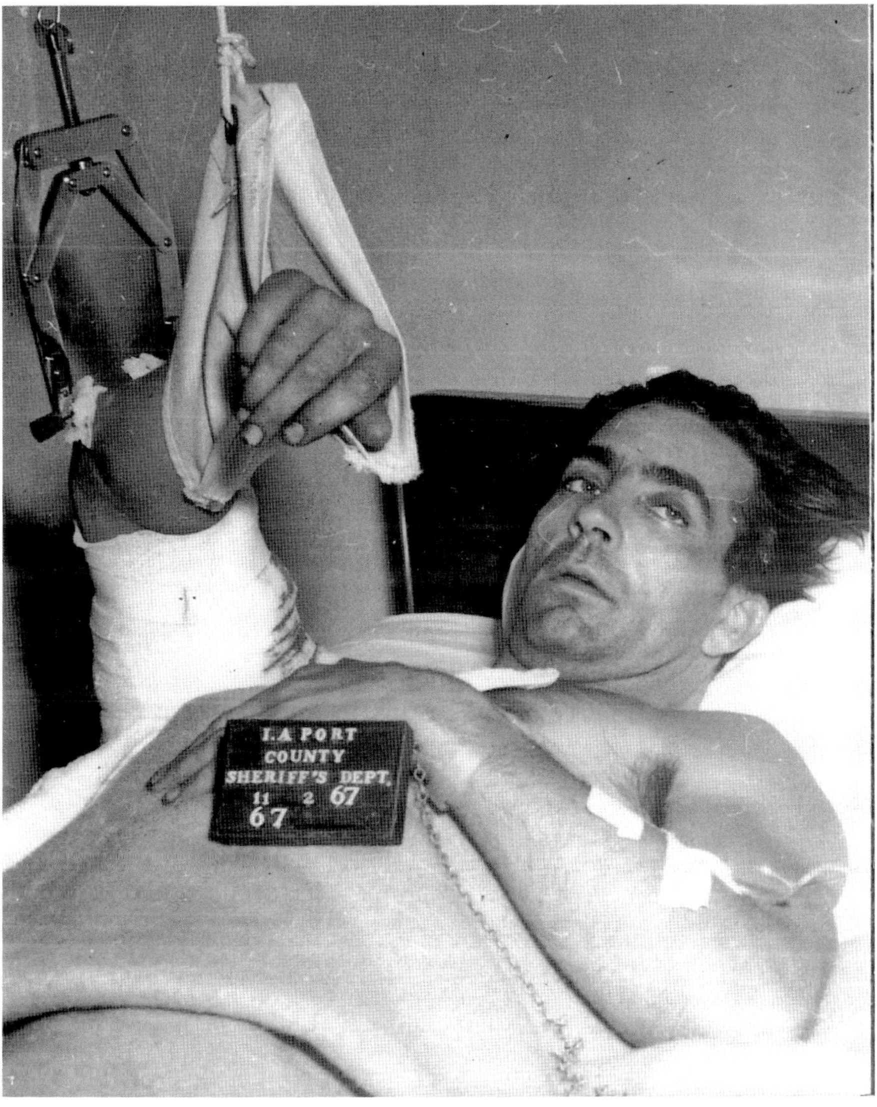

Henry Gargano in police custody after his arrest and subsequent surgery in La Porte County, Indiana, on November 2, 1967. *Courtesy of the Northlake Police Department.*

hung up the phone and contemplated the strange call for a moment. The bandits' run had come to an end, he figured. Somehow the authorities must have them cornered. Now they faced the justice system. After taking a deep breath, Dr. Howard picked up the phone, dialed the FBI's phone number and informed them of the only incident that had involved the blond-haired woman since the previous Saturday. The FBI promptly thanked him for the information and told him they would keep abreast of the situation. Dr. Howard then returned to tending to his patients and his own legal troubles.

Neither the names of the informants nor the names of the inmates who revealed vital clues to the FBI were ever disclosed. The FBI did a thorough investigation of Marion inmates as they made agreements with certain inmates for reduced sentences. That information has remained hidden. The unknown female informant was critical in piecing together the Bellwood hideout. The Marion inmate or inmates who shared Gargano's lifestyle and love interests provided invaluable information. The FBI conducted a thorough search of Monica Conner's Gold Coast apartment, which revealed clues about her and revealed the fact that there were some visitors in that apartment a few days prior to the search. Dr. Howard informed police authorities that the blond-haired woman arrived in a Checkered Cab seeking medical attention for her boyfriend. Police traced the cab's records to verify Monica Conner's apartment location, or at least to gather enough information to figure it out. This was simple and diligent police work.

ALL FOUR FUGITIVES were returned to Chicago. Gargano underwent surgery to repair his infected shoulder. Doctors mentioned there was a chance they would have to amputate. Only time would tell. He was transported via ambulance under heavy guard. Their return was ironic in many ways. During their escape to Indiana, they were discreet, almost paranoid. Multiple times Daniels and Annette had switched driving the getaway car. Their trip was under the darkness of night.

Yet one week later, the four of them were the most guarded persons in the country. Media attention swirled throughout the country regarding the Northlake Bank robbers. With their capture came an array of questions and doubts about the parole system, robberies and police response to bank alarms. They were the biggest news in the country for a week. As the ambulance drove on Interstate 94 with lights on, every vehicle saw it from miles away and realized that the long line of police vehicles was likely escorting the Northlake Bank robbers to Chicago on murder charges.

Chapter 5

LEGAL PROCEEDINGS

A month after the Northlake Bank robbers were charged in Indiana, the United States Supreme Court listened to a case that captured the division and sentiment concerning the death penalty. The Supreme Court listened to arguments on *United States v. Charles Jackson*, case number 390 US 570.[176] The United States Supreme Court, led by Chief Justice Earl Warren, was notorious for actively changing policy. Capital punishment was a divisive issue that the Warren-led Supreme Court addressed. For the Northlake Bank robbers' legal strategy, sentiment over the death penalty came at the perfect time.

Earl Warren was born on March 19, 1891, in Los Angeles to Norwegian and Swedish immigrants and raised in Bakersfield, California. In Bakersfield, Warren's father worked as a railroad car repairman on the Southern Pacific Railroad. Warren joined his father during summers as he worked on the railroads—a job he credited with developing his knowledge about working people and their problems. The observant Warren blamed government for the crime and vice of nearby saloons and brothels. After he left Bakersfield for Berkeley, Warren attended the University of California's undergraduate program and law school. He desired to work as an attorney.

Warren eventually became attorney general of California from 1938 until 1942 and then became governor of California. Warren served as California's governor for three terms. After he developed his skills as a politician, Warren's ambitions led him to seek higher office. Warren ran as the Republican vice presidential candidate with Thomas Dewey in 1948, losing to Democrat

Harry S. Truman. However, Warren and Dewey played vital roles in securing Dwight Eisenhower's Republican nomination. After Eisenhower became president, he appointed Warren to the Supreme Court as the chief justice. Questions quickly surfaced over Warren's academic abilities. Warren was more of a politician than an academic. His political abilities were evident, but his academic credentials were lacking. Using his skills as a politician, Warren smartly asked Justice Hugo Black to head the court while he familiarized himself with his responsibilities. The move proved vital as Warren demonstrated being a quick learner. The direction of the Supreme Court took a direct and important turn.

The Supreme Court reflected American sentiment heading into the tumultuous 1960s. There was a deep division between judicial activists and advocates for judicial restraint. Warren used his political abilities to establish himself as the court's leader. During his time as chief justice, Warren oversaw influential cases that affected American life for generations. Warren presided over the court as it decided the constitutionality of racial segregation. He wrote his opinion that "carefully distinguished between the principle that racial segregation violated the Equal Protection Clause and that remedies to his situation would be determined in the future."[177] The court's decision on *Brown v. Board of Education*, announced on May 17, 1954, held that racial segregation was unconstitutional, which triggered the civil rights movement. Up to that point, the court had dealt primarily with property rights and individual rights. Warren held that the Constitution gave the court sufficient authority to remedy injustice.

For the greater part of our nation's founding, the death penalty was generally accepted and enforced. Arguments in favor of the death penalty proceeded from the Fifth, Eighth and Fourteenth Amendments. The Fifth Amendment reads, "No person shall be held to answer for a capital, or otherwise infamous crime, unless on a presentment or indictment of a Grand Jury." The purpose of this amendment is to protect against unfair treatment in the legal process. The Eighth Amendment states, "Excessive bail shall not be required nor excessive fines imposed, nor cruel and unusual punishment." A person is protected from both the federal and state governments' imposing extreme punishment. The last significant amendment regarding the death penalty was the Fourteenth Amendment. The Fourteenth Amendment states that all persons born or naturalized in the United States have rights that the state cannot take away. Known as a Reconstruction Amendment, this amendment gave equal protection of the laws, particularly to former slaves.

The death penalty was protected under these amendments. However, interpretation of the Eighth Amendment shifted in 1958. The Warren Supreme Court's decision in *Trop v. Dulles* (1958) was that the interpretation of the Eighth Amendment contained an "evolving standard of decency that marked the progress of a maturing society." Death penalty abolitionists quickly argued that the United States' progression included a standard of decency that required the country to no longer implement the death penalty. The key to their argument was that if the United States continued to practice the death penalty, then it had not evolved, it had not progressed and it should not consider itself a mature society. Although *Trop v. Dulles* was not a death penalty case, the Warren Supreme Court introduced language that included "evolving," "progress" and "maturing society." These words shifted the focus. This language worked its way to district courts, influencing justices in some cases.

Death penalty discussion continued for most of the 1960s. As arguments surged regarding the language introduced into American society in the late 1950s, the Warren Supreme Court began to keenly discuss the administration of the death penalty. The Warren Supreme Court heard two cases in 1968 that dealt with the discretion given to the prosecutor and the jury in capital cases.

In the first case, the *United States v. Charles Jackson* (1968), the Supreme Court heard arguments on a federal kidnapping statute. The statute required that the death penalty be imposed only upon recommendation of a jury. The Warren Supreme Court was to decide whether defendants were likely encouraged to waive their rights to a jury trial in order to avoid the death sentence and if the practice of capital punishment was unconstitutional. If the only means of applying capital punishment was by recommendation of a jury and not by the court, then there was no incentive for defendants to ask for a jury trial in order to avoid the death penalty. Hence, the defendants' best interest was to waive a trial by jury, thus avoiding a death sentence since a judge could only sentence the defendants to life imprisonment.

In the case of the Northlake Bank robbers, their lawyers argued from precedent prior to the Supreme Court decision. The *Jackson* case was first heard in Connecticut in 1966, with a decision in 1967, prior to its hearing before the Supreme Court. Sentiment shifted among the public and among justices in lower courts. In early March 1968, lawyers' arguments were based on Connecticut chief justice Timbers's statement that the federal kidnapping act violated the Sixth Amendment rights of defendants who were ready to submit a plea. Essentially, the defendants could not freely exercise their Sixth Amendment right based on the potential risk that they might lose their lives.

The Northlake Bank robbers' attorneys felt this tactic was worth the effort. Divisive convictions in the public and among justices could potentially be vital. Those efforts were quickly exhausted. Illinois State Attorney Edward Hanrahan argued in favor of dismissing the defendants' right to waive a trial by jury. Too many cases surfaced in which the judge opposed the argument in the Connecticut case. Hanrahan listed these cases and argued that the trial judge could follow or disregard the jury's recommendation. The judge was not bound by the jury. A trial by jury and imposition of the punishment if found guilty were to be separated. One had no bearing on the other. The motion was eventually denied on April 2. Capital punishment's demise in general American sentiment, in the Warren Supreme Court's critical comments and in Connecticut's *Jackson* case prior to the hearing before the Supreme Court demonstrated its divisiveness. The lawyers searched for additional strategic moves.

THE SECOND CASE that had relevance to the capital punishment discussion of the 1960s was *Witherspoon v. Illinois*, case number 391 US 510. This case was argued on April 24, 1968, and decided on June 3, 1968. The discussion centered on a juror's reservations about the death penalty. A juror's reservations about the death penalty were not sufficient grounds to prevent that juror's service on a death penalty case. A juror could only be disqualified if prosecutors clearly demonstrated that the juror's view of the death penalty prevented him from making an impartial decision about punishment. A juror was to be impartial in deciding the case's punishment. So the case against the Northlake Bank robbers found itself in the midst of national debates on parole and the death penalty. General public sentiment wrestled over rehabilitated prisoners and the legitimacy of capital punishment.

IF ANY CASE MERITED the death penalty, the case against the Northlake Bank robbers in the spring of 1968 was the clear choice. The Northlake Bank robbers robbed a bank and murdered responding police officers using high-powered weapons. If these bandits did not receive the death penalty, the consensus was that no one would receive capital punishment. However, these two Supreme Court cases represented the shifting attitude against capital punishment. These case decisions clearly impacted the Northlake Bank robbers' strategy of avoiding the death penalty.

"A Fair and Impartial Jury..."

After their return to Chicago, the Northlake Bank robbers and their two female accomplices stood before Judge William J. Campbell, chief judge of the federal district court. Since they claimed they had no money to hire their own lawyers, they were given court-appointed lawyers as part of the federal defender program.

Clifton Daniels stood front and center before Judge Hubert L. Will, who filled in for the appointed judge, Edwin A. Robson, and pleaded innocent to aggravated bank robbery that resulted in the murder of two police officers. Daniels was then led in handcuffs and leg irons to an isolated cell in the maximum security section of the county jail. Daniels remained in jail as he heard about his court-appointed attorneys. Judge Campbell appointed two well-known and respected lawyers to the case. One was Terrence F. MacCarthy, director of the Federal Defender Program. The other lawyer, Thomas D. Decker, was deputy director of the program.

As a result of the intense media focus on the bank robbery, these two attorneys would likely receive much attention during the trial. Yet they were poised attorneys willing to work diligently to fulfill their responsibilities as leaders of the Federal Defender Program.

The Federal Defender Program was a result of the Criminal Justice Act of 1964. The purpose of the act was to ensure quality legal representation to all persons charged with a federal crime who did not have the financial means to pay for their own legal counsel. The federal courts made sixteen thousand compensated appointments of counsel in the first year.[178] Prior to the act, persons without financial ability to pay for their own counsel were the general responsibility of the bar. The courts, however, appointed unwilling or inexperienced lawyers without any compensation. The end result was inferior legal representation for poor criminals.

The goal of the Federal Defender Program was to provide quality legal representation for those charged with federal crimes. Clifton Daniels's main attorney was the newly appointed director of the Federal Defender Program, Terrence MacCarthy. MacCarthy was appointed director in 1966 by judges of the United States District Court and deans of the six Chicago law schools. He graduated from DePaul Law School in 1960 and served as Judge Campbell's law clerk and as Illinois special attorney general. His emphasis was primarily in criminal and civil trials. Terrence MacCarthy and

Thomas Decker's responsibility was to provide effective legal representation to Clifton Daniels, a man charged with federal crime but with no financial resources to pay for legal counsel. Ironically, Daniels was in possession of tens of thousands of dollars soon after the robbery, but now he could not pay for a lawyer.

ANNETTE GARGANO LEONARDO and Monica Florence Conner were also arraigned before Judge Campbell. Judge Campbell appointed to them James B. Sloan and Raymond Smith, both assistant United States attorneys. Judge Campbell's clear direction for the two lawyers was to file all pre-trial motions within twenty days. He gave the government fifteen days to respond, and he gave the defense lawyers five days to respond to the government—all guidelines to be followed strictly. The two women were given $10,000 bond each. They could go free by posting $1,000 cash each.

Judge Campbell assigned Judge Richard B. Austin as their trial judge.

THE TWO REMAINING defendants, Henry Gargano and Ronald Dale Raine, were not arraigned on the same day as the others. They remained under heavy guard at their respective hospitals. Gargano received further treatment for his arm wound after surgery. Police officers guarded Raine at Bridewell Hospital. Both of them were arraigned in December 1967.

Henry Gargano was assigned attorneys Edward Calihan and Ronald Alwin. Ronald Dale Raine was assigned Charles Bellows and Joseph Ettinger.

April 2, 1968

After weeks of additional strategizing, the defendants, along with their attorneys, again questioned a trial by jury. Their strategy and questioning focused on avoiding case prejudice. The case received massive pre-trial publicity. Newspaper articles were written. Parole board members spoke publicly. The lawyers argued that a fair and impartial jury could not be selected. The Northlake Bank robbery received national attention with major media outlets covering every angle of the robbery. No resident in the district could honestly state they remained unaffected by the media reports about the robbery. They had presuppositions set in their minds about each defendant and about the case in general. Too many opinions had been given that reached the general populace.

Judge Robson denied their motions to waive a public trial by jury. The death penalty debate raged on, and the Supreme Court was on the verge of giving a decision. To Judge Robson, the matter was already settled.

J. Howard Wood's FBI graduation speech a few months prior had touched on the topic of having an informed public and having a just and fair jury. The question resurfaced once more in this trial since the defendant's claim was that a fair and impartial jury could not be reached because of the massive pre-trial publicity, while the government's opinion was that a fair and impartial jury could be called regardless of the amount of pre-trial publicity. In order for a trial to be waived, the consent of the government had to be given, and the approval of the court before a defendant's rights to a fair and impartial jury had to be preserved.

The court's efforts focused on the amount of media coverage. The court's conclusion was that during the time of the crime and during the search for the Northlake Bank robbers, there was massive media coverage. Newspapers, magazines and other sources of media covered the story and provided details of the case that might have made an impartial jury impossible. However, the court's research found that since the defendant's arraignments, the publicity surrounding the Northlake Bank robbers had diminished significantly. Neither radio, television nor newspapers covered the defendants in similar fashion as during the manhunt. According to the court, only four small items related to the case appeared after November 13, 1967. The court's opinion was that the news media refrained from covering this story over such a significant period of time that a fair and impartial jury could be reached.

The court's appeal that a fair and impartial jury could be found was tied to the 1966 case of *Shepard v. Maxwell.* In that case, the defendant, Sam Sheppard, was publicly exposed prior to trial. Sam Sheppard's interrogation was on television, unfounded rumors grabbed headlines during his trial and the press dictated the amount of information released from the trial to the public. The judge's control was not evident during the trial. The media supplanted the judge as the authoritative force. The judge never issued a continuance.

According to the court, if there was doubt about having a fair and impartial jury, several steps were to be taken. The recommended step was to issue a continuance. The amount of media coverage had subsided significantly since the bandits were arraigned. With a continuance, more time would have lapsed between the massive publicity and the trial.

However, the court's conviction was that even in the spring of 1968, a fair and impartial jury could be found. The court's intent was to proceed with a trial in September 1968, a full ten months after the Northlake Bank robbers were captured.

April 8, 1968[179]

The Warren Supreme Court's decision on *United States v. Charles Jackson*, case number 390 US 570, was decided. It reversed Connecticut's district court decision. The Supreme Court's introduction of language in regard to the death penalty years prior penetrated earlier courts, thus creating loopholes in certain cases for a period of time. Alert attorneys utilized these loopholes for their benefit. The Northlake Bank robbers tried unsuccessfully.

The original thought as stated in violation of the Federal Kidnapping Act was that "the Act was unconstitutional because by authorizing only the jury to impose the death penalty it makes 'the risk of death' the price for asserting the right to jury trial."[180] The Warren Supreme Court reversed its decision on direct appeal. Justice Potter Stewart expressed the opinion of six justices in stating that "the death penalty provision was invalid because [of its] imposing an impermissible burden upon any accused's exercise of this Fifth Amendment right not to plead guilty and his Sixth Amendment right to demand a jury trial, but that the remainder of the statute was valid, since the death penalty provision was severable from it."[181] The reversal of that decision struck down the provision that authorized only the jury to impose the death penalty.

Two dissenting justices, Hugo Black and Byron White, disagreed on "the grounds that the statute may be properly interpreted so as to avoid constitutional questions, and thus that the judgment should be reversed, making it clear that pleas of guilty and waivers of jury trials should be carefully examined before they are accepted."[182] A third justice, Thurgood Marshall, the nation's first African American justice, did not participate in the vote.

Justice Stewart stated that the law itself should not be invalidated in its entirety "simply because its capital punishment clause violates the Constitution."[183] Justice Stewart's opinion went further on the topic of capital punishment by stating, "A defendant who elects to be tried by a jury cannot be put to death even if the jury so recommends—unless the trial judge agrees that capital punishment should be imposed."[184] The trial judge and the jury had to agree that the case merits capital punishment. Stewart then opined, "Moreover, the argument goes, a defendant cannot avoid the risk of death by attempting to plead guilty or waive a jury trial."[185] The main emphasis was that the death penalty may only be imposed "if and only if both judge and jury concur in its imposition."[186]

Justice Stewart then stated, "Under the Federal Kidnapping Act, therefore, the defendant who abandons the right to contest his guilt before a jury is assured that he cannot be executed."[187] So in the case of the Northlake Bank robbers, under the previous provision of the Federal Kidnapping Act, they were highly encouraged to abandon their right to contest their guilt before a jury in order to avoid the death penalty. If their trial therefore never went before the jury, then they did not qualify for capital punishment.

The Northlake Bank robbers' initial intent was to avoid a trial by jury based on violation of free exercise of their Sixth Amendment rights and then on the lack of an impartial jury. Their motions were denied. One last incident changed the direction of their lawyers' strategies. After that incident, the lawyers for the Northlake Bank robbers suggested they plead guilty, placing their lives in the judge's hand. Eventually that decision removed the possibility of a death sentence since there would be no jury. The judge could only sentence the defendants to maximum imprisonment. Their next pre-trial hearing came on July 16, 1968.

Late Spring 1968

As time approached for them to present themselves before Judge Robson on July 16, 1968, the three Northlake Bank robbers were led to Marshall's offices in the Dirksen Federal Building. Although Gargano, Raine and Daniels saw one another in the county jail, their relationship was very different in prison than it was on the outside. There were no more seemingly limitless amounts of money, no more drinking, no more girls, no more 606 Club. With the exception of planned "free times" in prison, they spent the majority of their time in prison cells—nothing glamorous. However, in late May and early June, the three bandits concocted yet another ploy.

Gargano continually voiced his displeasure of spending time behind prison walls. That was no life for him. He had spent the majority of his life in the custody of law enforcement ever since he was in the reformatory in St. Charles. That's all he'd ever known—enough was enough. Gargano quietly spoke to Raine and Daniels about one last "heist"—except this was no bank robbery heist.

In prison, inmates meet an array of people with a variety of skills. Prisoners consist of people who are good at working with their hands, people who are good at scheming and devising plans and people who are good at working with keys and locks, such as Raine. Gargano, excited about the possibility of being free once more, talked with fellow inmates about concealing a weapon when they went to the courthouse. Upon being transferred to the courtroom, they would break themselves free. Rumors quickly circulated. Inmates talked, discussed and shared with one another to see if the Northlake Bank robbers would be able to strike once more.

However, for every inmate faithful to fellow prisoners, a few were more loyal to their own cause of getting out of jail sooner rather than later. As news circulated once more about the Northlake Bank robbers, one inmate sought a different opportunity—to get out of prison early. He worked his deal with the warden as an informant.

Warden Winston Moore learned from his informant in mid-June that the Northlake Bank robbers planned to escape.[188] They would try at the time of the court appearance a month later, in mid-July.

Gargano's prison connections enabled him to obtain a gun. An Italian-made revolver to be exact. The gun was a snub-nose revolver that he admired. Prison was similar to the outside. It was all about your connections. Gargano, still with a cast on his right arm from the gunshot wound, hid the weapon in his cast. The cops could do a strip search on him but would not find his weapon.

Daniels, on the other hand, had weeks to sharpen a knife. He worked on the table knife for a few weeks while locked up in his cell. As the lights dimmed, Daniels pulled his knife out, used some homemade tools and sharpened it. However, Daniels did not have a cast to conceal his weapon. He found another way to smuggle the table knife.

July 16, 1968

Gargano, Raine and Daniels were transferred from the county jail to the Dirksen Federal Building early that day. Prior to getting out of the van,

Warden Moore, relying on his informant, ordered an extensive search of all three men. Moore personally supervised the search. Gargano was given a pat down that went from his shoulders to his torso, to his waist and down his legs. He came up with nothing. Warden Moore found that odd.

Daniels was next. The officers did the same procedure as on Gargano. They searched Daniels from the top of his body all the way to the bottom for weapons—nothing. Warden Moore thought it was likely Raine who would bring the weapons.

Raine was searched like the other two. Their search yielded the same result: nothing. Since their search was concluded, the three prisoners were taken to Dirksen Federal Building temporary cells. Warden Moore's suspicion continued. He kept a close eye on all three of them.

As the three Northlake Bank robbers waited, their lawyers gathered inside Judge Robson's courthouse for a pre-trial hearing. The three lawyers conveyed to Judge Robson that there was no change in the status of their clients. The court's decision was to have the case go to trial, and the court was to have jurors called so they could proceed with the trial on September 9, 1968, at 10:00 a.m. In closing the pre-trial hearing, Judge Robson stated that "arrangements will be made by the marshal to bring in the prisoners on Tuesday, a week from today, so that they can be interviewed by counsel."[189] Everything proceeded as planned.

However, the three bank robbers' status quickly changed. Alone, Daniels quickly pulled out a table knife and handed it to Raine. Daniels had sneaked the knife in from the county jail this far, but he was apprehensive about going through with it. He had no way to further conceal the knife. Raine's adrenaline for another action-packed day simmered. Raine held Daniels's knife with the handle rightly positioned in his coat pocket. The plan was to wait for Gargano's next step.

Gargano pulled the gun out of his cast and slid it into his waistband. Gargano knew that he couldn't take the risk of fumbling around for a weapon deeply hidden in his cast. The officers came to their cell, ready to transfer the three bandits to Judge Robson's federal courthouse. In their lawyer's viewpoint, the three would plead not guilty and wait for trial by a jury.

During their moment in the cell, as they waited for their court appearance, the agents prepared to transfer the Northlake Bank robbers. The bandits were under the authority of Marshal Joseph Tierney. Warden Moore distrusted the three bandits. His informants were reliable—usually. Warden

Moore talked to Marshal Tierney, relaying his informant's message that the three planned an escape. Marshal Tierney then ordered another search. His marshals searched all three men again prior to their transfer to the courthouse.

The agents first led Gargano out of the marshal's office. As Gargano was searched, a federal agent started his patdown from the top of the shoulders—nothing. He then moved his hands to the torso—nothing. As he moved his right hand around Gargano's waist, he surprisingly felt something. Upon a closer look, he noticed a bulge in Gargano's waistband. His initial reaction was to take Gargano down to the ground and subdue him. The federal agent then grabbed the weapon as he yelled to other law enforcement officials near him. Nearby officers quickly rushed to the remaining two prisoners, took them down to the ground and searched them thoroughly. An agent pointed his shotgun directly at Raine. Raine's search led to a sharpened table knife in his pocket.

Chaos ensued as agents rushed over to Daniels. They took him down, searched him thoroughly and did not find anything.

Judge Edwin Robson was sitting on his bench at 3:00 p.m. later that afternoon. The clerk initiated the session: "Your Honor, it has been requested to recall the case that was scheduled for this morning."[190] Terrence MacCarthy, lawyer for Clifton Daniels, spoke next. "Let the record show that the three defendants and their counsel are here present in court. On behalf of the defendant Daniels, Your Honor, we would like to withdraw the plea of not guilty heretofore entered and substitute in lieu thereof a plea of guilty."[191] MacCarthy quickly acknowledged that he advised his client, Daniels, of the possible penalty in the case, of his right to trial and a trial by jury to determine his guilt or innocence. However, "it is his desire to withdraw his plea of not guilty and to enter a plea of guilty at this time."[192]

Judge Robson then asked, "You have advised him that it is a minimum of ten years with no maximum sentence, is that right?"[193]

MacCarthy responded, "I have, your honor."[194]

Lawyers for the other two defendants also entered guilty pleas for their clients. Their strategy to have a trial failed with that morning's events. Judge Robson read the indictment charges of taking approximately $83,783 from the Northlake Bank and thereafter killing Northlake police officers John Nagle and Anthony Perri in violation of Title 18, United States Code, Section 2113 (e). Judge Robson asked each defendant directly if he desired to withdraw his plea of not guilty and enter a plea of guilty. All three defendants responded in the affirmative.

After a brief recess, everyone reconvened at 4:00 p.m. for immediate sentencing. John Conlon, assistant U.S. attorney, read over the case before recommending sentencing. Conlon stated, "It is the government's contention that the penalty which is provided and which is set down could be up to 199 years, the statute providing not less than ten years…because of the coldblooded and calculated manner in which they executed this crime, the government believes that a sentence of 199 years is necessary just because of the facts."[195] Conlon continued, "We know that there are many references to the fact that 199 years is an impossible term to serve, that generally this means only 40 years, but we believe that a sentence of 199 years would indicate to any parole board that these men should never be released again."[196] The government laid out its case before the court regarding sentencing. Before the sentencing, though, another presentation was to take place.

Judge Robson stated that the court was incorporating a psychological evaluation of the defendants. Arnold Abrams, the consulting psychologist, began with Daniels. Abrams said, "The central theme which runs through much of Daniels' psychological production is paranoia. Daniels' lifetime adaptation is to regard all persons, including those who are close to him, with extreme suspicion and distrust. Daniels has very fundamental difficulty in relating to women and tends to either deny his needs in this area or act aggressively when his emotions are aroused."[197]

Abrams added that because of "Daniels' guardedness, caution and suspicions, he does not permit himself to get close to people and as a result of this one sees a good deal of starvation for affection and nourishment."[198] MacCarthy requested that his incarceration begin immediately.

The next defendant to step forward was Ronald Dale Raine. Abrams began, "Raine showed a rather compulsive concern with sexuality. This may, in part, reflect lack of fulfillment in his life in this area. He has many irrational fears and phobias which are utilized to deal with his anxiety. Despite his verbalized concern with humanity in the abstract, there is evidence that he can be quite vengeful and sadomasochistic behavior is very much a part of his style of life. In line with this he literally appeared to be in a pathological way pleased at being caught, injured and subjected to imprisonment at the time of the trial."[199] Raine's attorney, Joseph Ettinger, also requested that sentencing for his client start immediately.

The last person to be evaluated was Henry Gargano. Abram remarked that suicide entered Gargano's mind several times, but Gargano "really did not think he could take his own life. He said that his family would probably be better off if he were executed. He depicted his background as one of marginal economic existence and laid the blame for his behavior on circumstances."[200] Abrams continued, "The Court would be remiss in its responsibility to the community if it did not impose the maximum sentence."[201] Attorney Edward Calihan simply inquired of the judge if his client's sentencing would begin immediately. Judge Robson quickly answered, "Yes."[202]

SINCE THEIR ARREST in Indiana in December, the Northlake Bank robbers had been held at the county jail in Chicago under Warden Winston Moore. Upon the recent attempt to break out of jail, Judge Robson decided to immediately send them to federal prison. Judge Robson affirmed, "The Court has already directed the marshal to make immediate arrangements to take each of the defendants here to a proper place of imprisonment, one of the federal penitentiaries. That will be commenced today."[203] Gargano, Raine and Daniels were no longer inmates at the county jail. They now belonged to the federal system. Their permanent home would likely be Marion Federal Penitentiary in downstate Illinois.

Un-rehabilitated Prisoners

Marion Federal Penitentiary was built in 1963, a few years prior to the Northlake Bank robbery. Marion replaced Alcatraz, the famous federal prison off the shores of San Francisco. Marion's initial population was primarily composed of transfers from Alcatraz. The prison held approximately five hundred of the most dangerous inmates, sufficient reason to provide maximum security. Marion Federal Penitentiary remained the country's most secure prison for years. Every prisoner who registered into the prison remained there. Breaking out of Marion was simply too daunting a task. Gargano's escapades of absolute freedom beyond Marion came to a close. His days involved primarily sitting in a cell as part of the solitary confinement program.

In 1973, Marion Federal Penitentiary installed the first blocks of its control-unit cells. The electronic age had come to Marion. Gargano, now serving his fifth year, desired evermore to taste freedom once more.

Ronald Dale Raine's sentence was initiated at the Leavenworth Penitentiary in Kansas. With much time on his hands, Raine focused on activism in prison. From 1968 to 1973, during his time in Leavenworth, Raine researched prisoner rights. That period resulted in lawsuits filed over the course of his imprisonment. Ever involved, Raine also participated in activism that resulted in disciplinary action. The final straw was in 1972, when Raine was placed in solitary confinement without a hearing for supposedly leading a prison strike of Mexican American prisoners. Raine denied involvement in that strike. His hatred of law enforcement became vivid as he argued prisoners' violation of rights in solitary confinement without a hearing.

Shortly thereafter, Raine was temporarily transferred to a segregated facility at a federal prison in Springfield, Missouri. From there, Raine was sent to Marion Federal Penitentiary, where the control-unit cells were installed in 1973. He was now reunited with his former crime partner Henry Michael Gargano.

Daniels's incarceration took him through several federal penitentiaries. Unlike his fellow cohorts, Daniels's life in prison remained relatively quiet and peaceful. He spent three years in Marion until 1983, before being transferred to Leavenworth for a brief stint. From there, Daniels spent nine years in Terre Haute Federal Penitentiary, a high-security penitentiary near the Illinois-Indiana border. After Terre Haute, Daniels was moved to Oxford Federal Correctional Institution, about sixty miles north of Madison, Wisconsin. He would serve his last years of incarceration at a regular prison facility in Oxford.

In August 1999, Daniels complained of pain and was taken to a local hospital. He would soon be transferred to FMC Rochester in Minnesota, a federal medical center.

Aiding, Abetting and Harboring

Winter 1967–1968

After the capture of the bank robbers, Annette Leonardo and Monica Conner were charged with "assisting bank robbers with intent to thereby prevent their apprehension, trial and punishment."[204] For the next year, both women had pre-trial hearings. Monica Conner's lawyer argued for leniency in light of her testimony the night of her capture. After all, she solely cooperated with authorities.

Annette never cooperated with authorities. She revered her relationship with her brother more than cooperating with authorities. She took that risk.

Both women initially pleaded not guilty to the charges.

After further investigation, authorities learned that the woman driving the vehicle that blocked the intersection of Lavergne Avenue and Westward Ho Drive was Jean Gargano, sister-in-law to Henry Gargano. She was charged with "aiding and harbouring wanted criminals."[205] Jean was the woman in the backseat of the getaway car that assisted Henry Gargano as they drove through from Northlake to Bellwood. The worker at the Leyden Medical Center noticed a woman sitting in the backseat. That woman was indeed Jean Gargano. Soon after their arrival in Bellwood, Jean departed the group. She never fired a gun. She simply aided two criminals and harbored them for a few hours.

November 19, 1968

After initially pleading not guilty to their charges, Annette Leonardo and Monica Conner pleaded guilty before Judge Richard Austin. Monica Conner's lawyer argued in favor of Monica's cooperation with authorities the night she was arrested. Monica Conner was "sentenced to one-year probation."[206] Her probation requirement included periodic registration with a probation officer. That night's cooperation was the difference.

Annette was a different matter. After she pleaded guilty, Judge Austin sentenced her to "a year in prison…in federal district court for aiding and abetting the escape of two men convicted of killing two policemen."[207] Annette served her sentence in a minimum-security prison for female offenders in West Virginia.

In April 1969, she wrote a letter to Judge Austin asking for reduction in sentence. Her daughter had suffered an accident and partially burned her face. Judge Austin denied her motion.

January 1969

Jean Gargano pleaded guilty to the charges of aiding and harboring. Jean gave first aid to Henry Gargano after he received a bullet wound to the shoulder. Jean's four-month sentence was served at the Community Treatment Center in Chicago's downtown YMCA hotel. During her sentence, she attended "beautician's school during the day, but returned to the hotel each night."[208] Jean returned to her Chicago-area home after she served her sentence.

EPILOGUE

Henry Gargano, the reputed leader of the Northlake Bank robbers, quietly remained in Marion from 1973 until 1975. In October 1975, opportunity knocked once more. Marion's highly touted electronic system was the means to break out. Gargano's fellow inmate worked as an electrician, responsible for working on the prison's lock mechanisms. Over time, he simply collected the materials needed to create a remote control that opened the prison's doors and gates.

On Friday evening, October 10, 1975, Gargano and seventeen other inmates attended a meeting of the prison's historical society. A Southern Illinois University professor and five students made their presentation to the inmates. As the meeting progressed, one prisoner approached the university professor, showed him a cut on his finger and asked for a Band-Aid. The inmate followed the willing professor to the storage room in search of that Band-Aid. As the two men were inside the storage area, a second inmate walked briskly toward them. Once inside, both inmates overpowered the university professor, took his keys and locked him in the storage area. As they walked out of the storage room, the two inmates signaled to their willing partners. All five inmates walked rapidly out of that corridor, opened "two interior gates leading to the reception room at the prison front door" with the "homemade" electronic device and ran from Marion Federal Penitentiary.[209] For the first time in its eleven-year history, Marion had its first prison escapees—and the dangerous Henry Gargano was on the loose.

EPILOGUE

As the five inmates made their way about twenty miles south of Marion to Buncombe, Illinois, nearly two hundred FBI, state and local officials searched for them. Upon coming to a rural home in Buncombe, the five inmates scouted the premises and held the elderly couple there hostage for five hours. The group ate, changed clothing and stole the couple's vehicle before making their way to Salem, Illinois, on Sunday. Armed with the elderly couple's twenty-gauge shotgun and .22-caliber rifle, the inmates prepared to fight rather than spend more time in prison. Near Salem, a police officer noticed the five men, chased them in their vehicle and shot at them. The vehicle crashed, and the inmates scattered. An injured inmate was the only one captured at the scene. The other four fled in different directions.

Two of the remaining four inmates were captured on Monday, October 13. Gargano, however, made his way to Bloomfield, Indiana, where he was apprehended the following day, on Tuesday. At the local jail, the sheriff's wife spoke with Gargano, gave him a copy of the New Testament and tried to convince him to change his life. Gargano later stated, "In appreciation to the decent and humane treatment from all the people of the Greene County Jail…my particular regards to Marge Byers, whose interest and compassion will always be in my thoughts. If I ever do come to accept Jesus, it will be through Marge's doing. I say this in sincerity."[210] Gargano was returned to Marion Federal Penitentiary.

After repeated prison escapes in 1978 and 1985, Gargano added another citation to his prison record. In 2000, Henry Gargano was cited for marijuana possession. He also granted a rare interview in 1981. After he was asked if he felt remorse for the 1967 shooting, Gargano answered, "I don't feel any remorse about those dead cops…when you get hit or you hit someone in a shootout, that's a fair confrontation, like in Viet Nam…it can't be helped."[211]

Gargano's main contribution to those outside prison came in 1976, when he wrote a brief guide to prison slang. He explained such word as "shanks," "kites" and "fever."[212]

IN JANUARY 2010, the U.S. Parole Commission set Gargano's parole date for September 3, 2010. Gargano's intentions were to live the rest of his days with his sister in Illinois. Upon hearing about the commission's plans, Northlake police chief Norm Nissen and Officer John Nagle's family members rose up against that decision and requested that Gargano's parole be denied. Petitions were signed. The media focused on Gargano one last time. In March 2011, the parole commission denied Gargano's parole.

EPILOGUE

On October 13, 2011, the seventy-nine-year-old Henry Michael Gargano died at the federal medical center in Butner, North Carolina. After spending nearly a year at the medical center, Gargano succumbed to the complications of emphysema and two heart attacks. He never expressed remorse for his actions.

As for Ronald Dale Raine, he continued with his prison activism. Raine wrote about inadequate prison conditions and eventually became known as a "jailhouse lawyer." During his time in Marion Federal Penitentiary, Raine quickly picked up a reputation for a certain craft: locksmithing. An assistant to Marion's warden, John Clark, mentioned Ronald Dale Raine's name as one of the most dangerous inmates and most likely to escape. "He's one of the most dangerous escape artists in captivity…he's had a lengthy history of attempted escapes."[213] Raine built a reputation as a locksmith genius with an uncanny ability to duplicate keys from simple materials, such as plastic cups.

Raine filed lawsuits several times, notably against Marion's leadership for prison civil rights abuses. Following the publicized 1983 murder of two Marion corrections officers, Marion was placed on permanent lockdown. According to Raine, prisoners were stripped, beaten and abused during their cell searches, including rectal searches. Prisoners spent the majority of their days in their own cells with rare outside contact.

Like Gargano, Raine unsuccessfully attempted to escape prison in 1976 and 1982. He received extended solitary confinement for his efforts.

Raine was eventually transferred to a high-security prison in Florence, Colorado. His parole hearing was held on October 20, 2010. Again, Northlake police chief Norm Nissen and Officer John Nagle's family worked diligently to stop Raine's parole. Less than three weeks later, the U.S. Parole Commission followed a hearing examiner's recommendation and denied parole to Ronald Dale Raine. Just like Gargano, Raine was eligible for parole every two years. His next chance for parole was 2012.

Ronald Dale Raine died in prison on May 27, 2012, from a stroke. He never had his second parole hearing.

Clifton Orneal Daniels lived the last moments of his life more as a patient than as a prisoner. On Wednesday, September 1, 1999, Daniels, age sixty, died of cancer in the federal medical center in Rochester, Minnesota.[214] He never had a parole hearing.

In 1971, Northlake's city council voted to dedicate a park to their fallen heroes. Council members decided on a park near the town's center to serve

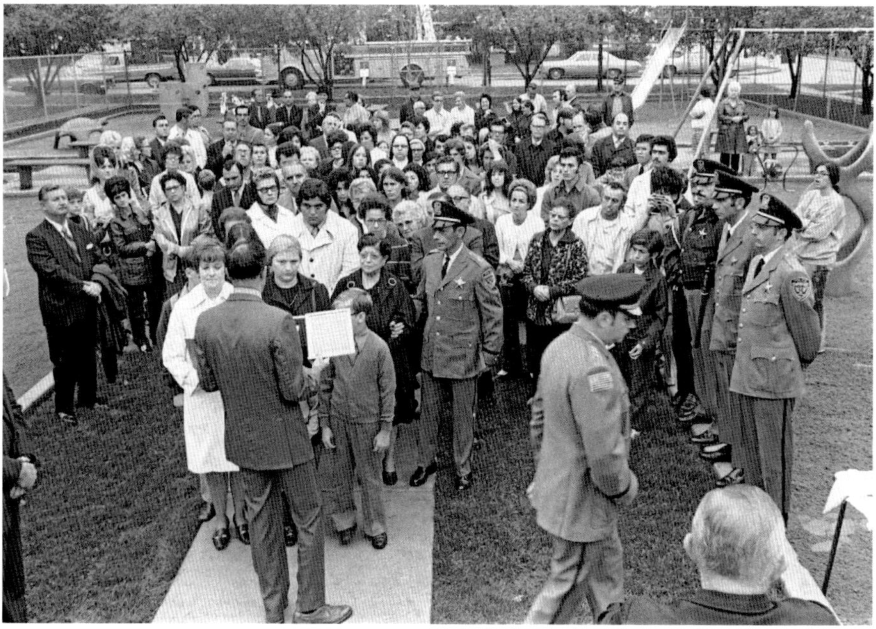

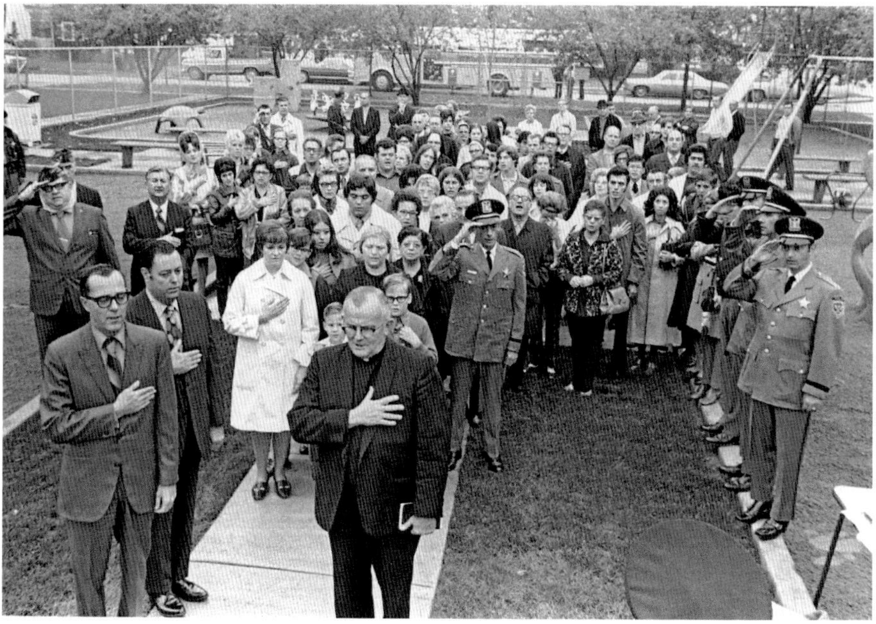

The Nagle and Perri families gather together to recognize the sacrifice of John Nagle and Anthony Perri at the 1971 dedication of Nagle-Perri Park as Officer Hustedt is present. A Catholic priest stands in the front as the Pledge of Allegiance is recited. *Courtesy of Northlake City Hall.*

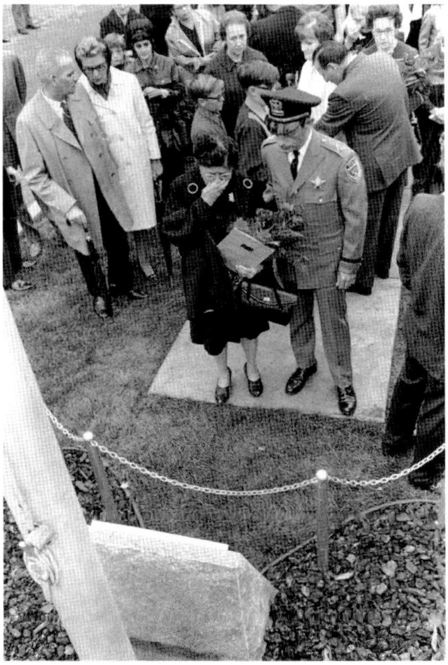

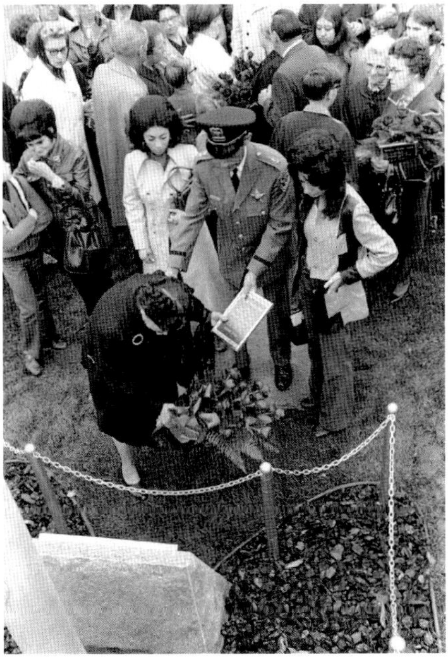

Antoinette Perri sheds tears at the 1971 dedication of Nagle-Perri Park as she reminisces the events of October 27, 1967. She also places a wreath of flowers at the plaque. *Courtesy of the Northlake City Hall.*

as a remembrance of the tragic events of October 27, 1967. The Nagle and Perri families united one last time as Officer Hustedt presented them with a plaque honoring Officers John J. Nagle and Anthony P. Perri. A priest offered warm words and faithful prayers to the mourning families.

Antoinette Perri's tearful eyes flowed once more as she placed flowers near the plaque at the base of the American flag. That plaque continues to remind Northlake residents of their own police heroes who died serving and protecting this community. As children frolic on park grounds, they read the plaque's words as many people have done for decades and will continue to do for decades to come.

ACKNOWLEDGEMENTS

The list of people to thank in helping this project along is lengthy. My research initially began at the National Archives and Records Administration Office in Chicago. The staff there provided insightful comments and assistance as needed. I remember the first time the cart with official court documents was brought to me—it seemed overwhelming. Staff members quickly added that I could take images of the files or use a flatbed scanner, thus making my job much easier. Thanks!

In addition, the Harold Washington Library was invaluable in providing newspaper articles. It was usually just me and a few other researchers glaring intently at the screen as we read dozens of articles in a single sitting, each doing his own "research." I have to admit that my experience here did not come without some adventures, such as the printer running out of ink; in my efforts to fix my problem, I smeared ink all over my hands and subsequently my pants. I quickly walked to the bathroom with my backpack hanging below my waist to conceal my embarrassment. As it turns out, nothing soap and water couldn't fix!

The staff at the Northlake Public Library was also very helpful. In their stacks, they pulled several local newspapers and news bulletins that gave me insight into local residents' thoughts during that hectic day and its aftermath. I've garnered great respect for local libraries as they preserve local history, thus linking current residents with their neighborhood's past. I hope local libraries continue to serve as this bridge.

As for individuals, there are plenty to thank. A good friend and former editor, Ted Griffin, was kind enough to look over my manuscript and its many errors. He kindly fit me into his busy schedule. Whatever mistakes I made are a result of my own shortcomings and not a reflection of his editing skills. Also, the Northlake police chief, Norm Nissen Jr., provided several invaluable meetings, giving me insights into the case and sharing important information that was not made available to the public. His father was very active in this case decades back, and I greatly benefitted from his insight.

Furthermore, in gathering newspaper articles and information on the Northlake Bank Robbers, reference librarians at local libraries were of tremendous help. Staff members at libraries in Canton, Ohio; downstate Illinois; Yakima, Washington; and southeastern Michigan were extremely generous with their time. To you, I say, "Thank you!"

In addition, I hope these research and writing projects inspire the local Latino community to read, research and learn about their local communities, as each Chicago suburb is rich with history. As a Mexican American, I know the important role of history in our lives, and I hope that we treasure our history as we continue to integrate in this country.

My hope is also that younger relatives such as my niece, Meghan, develop a thirst for writing well. As I develop my writing, I've realized the importance of this skill—may she also treasure its importance. May this book encourage her as she encourages me with her world travels.

Most importantly, I am grateful to the Lord for wonderful parents. When I decided to work on this project, I knew the great undertaking it would be for my initial book. My parents graciously rearranged the dining room, and I eventually made it into my personal office space. The dining table continued to be littered with articles, binders and personal notes as I furiously read and typed my manuscript. Without them, I could not have finished this project or any other project thus far in my life. Thank you!

NOTES

Chapter 1: Rehabilitated Prisoners

1. *Chicago Sun-Times*, "FBI Chief Raps Parole Setup," 34.
2. J. Edgar Hoover, FBI speech 1244059-0 001 HQ 101 60, FBI Graduation speech, November 2, 1967, 1.
3. Thomas Reddin, FBI speech 1244059-0 001 HQ 101 60, FBI Graduation speech, November 2, 1967, 3.
4. Ibid.
5. Ibid., 8.
6. Ibid.
7. J. Howard Wood, FBI speech 1244059-0 001 HQ 101 60, FBI Graduation speech, November 2, 1967, 2.
8. Ibid., 5.
9. Ibid., 7.
10. Ibid., 7–8.
11. Associated Press, "Defends U.S. Parole," 5.
12. Ibid.
13. Ibid.
14. Ibid.
15. Fulwood, "History of the Federal Parole System."
16. Grossman, Keating and Reiff, *Encyclopedia of Chicago*. The United Biscuit Company was renamed the Keebler Company in the 1960s, after first moving to Melrose Park, Illinois, and then to Elmhurst, Illinois.

17. Malby, "Willow Creek Boy." The majority of these comments were taken from Ronald Dale Raine's obituary.
18. Ibid., 1.

Chapter 2: October 27, 1967

19. Prentice, "Widows Grieve," 4.
20. Ibid.
21. Wolfe, "Policemen's Wives Tell of Worrying," 1–2.
22. Prentice, "Widows Grieve," 4.
23. Wolfe, "Policemen's Wives Tell of Worrying," 1–2.
24. Ibid.
25. Ibid.
26. Ibid.
27. St. John Chrysostom was founded in 1962 as a result of the overcrowding at a nearby parish, St. Simeon. About eight hundred families and five hundred children made the transition, demonstrating both the growth of the town and its youthfulness.
28. Prentice, "Widows Grieve."
29. Wolfe, "Policemen's Wives Tell of Worrying," 1–2.
30. Ibid.
31. Daniels, Confession.
32. See Malby, "Willow Creek Boy."
33. Daniels, Confession.
34. Thomson, "How Violence Built Up," 5.
35. See Malby, "Willow Creek Boy," 1.
36. Raine, "Casing the Joint."
37. Daniels, Confession.
38. Thomson, "How Violence Built Up," 5.
39. Court Transcripts of Proceedings, U.S. Northern District, Eastern Division, Case 67CR611 Edwin Robson, July 16, 1968, 20.
40. FBI report, 60.
41. Thomson, "How Violence Built Up," 5.
42. Ibid.
43. According to the assistant vice-president of the bank, George Ramsay, each teller's cage likely had more than $10,000 cash.
44. Daniels, Confession.
45. FBI Identification Division, FBI File No. 91-28365, 29.

46. Daniels, Confession.
47. FBI I Identification Division, FBI File No. 91-28365, 29.
48. Thomson, "How Violence Built Up," 5.
49. Drummond, "Officer," 1.
50. Gregory and Hinkle, "After 43 Years," 1.
51. Ibid.
52. Whisler, "Nation-wide Alert Ordered," 3.
53. Gregory and Hinkel, "After 43 Years," 1.
54. Court Transcripts of Proceedings, U.S. Northern District, Eastern Division, 67CR611, July 16, 1968.
55. Raine, "Casing the Joint."
56. Stumer, "Pathological Report and Protocol," 1967.
57. Casey and DeMuth, "Hunt Bank Killers," 1, 6.
58. Raine, "Casing the Joint." The authorities provided a false witness of Gargano running up to Perri and shooting him at close range. He stated there was no witness willing to stand there and see the entire incident as bullets were fired at an intense level. Perri was struck from the plethora of shots fired. Officer Bartkavich, though, stated that he clearly saw a man standing over an officer shooting at him. Raine was likely lying on the ground from the bullet that pierced his neck when this event occurred. Gargano vehemently denied this interpretation of events throughout his incarceration.
59. Kearns, "Pathological Report and Protocol," 1967.
60. DeMuth and Casey, "Hunt Bank Killers," 1, 6.
61. Ibid.
62. Thomson, "How Violence Built Up," 5.
63. Watson, "10:41 A.M.," 12.
64. Thomson, "How Violence Built Up," 5.
65. Watson, "10:41 A.M.," 12.
66. DeMuth and Casey, "Hunt Bank Killers of Two Cops," 6.
67. Daniels, Confession.
68. Whisler, "Nation-wide Alert Ordered," 3.
69. Ibid.
70. Daniels, Confession.
71. Thomson, "How Violence Built Up," 5.
72. DeMuth and Casey, "Hunt Bank Killers of Two Cops," 4–5.
73. Thomson, "How Violence Built Up," 5.
74. Daniels, Confession.
75. FBI I Identification Division, FBI File No. 91-28365, 83.

76. DeMuth and Casey, "Hunt Bank Killers of Two Cops," 4–5.
77. Watson, "10:41 A.M.," 12.
7878. Ibid.
79. Ibid.
80. Federal Bureau of Investigation, "A Brief History."
81. Ibid.
82. DeMuth and Casey, "Hunt Bank Killers of Two Cops," 1, 6.
83. FBI I Identification Division, FBI File No. 91-28365, 159–62. Raine would make this statement on November 3, 1967, but he continually refused to give additional information to law enforcement officials during his stay in the hospital.
84. Petacque, "FBI Identifies 2 Men," 42.
85. According to Cook County Sheriff's Office, cookcountysheriff.org.
86. Gregory and Hinkel, "After 43 Years," 1.
87. Casey and DeMuth, "Hunt Bank Killers of Two Cops," 6.
88. Ibid., 6.
89. Watson, "10:41 A.M.," 12.
90. Court Transcripts of Proceedings, US District Court for the Northern District of Illinois, Eastern Division, 1968, 27.
91. Granger, "Services Are Set," 2.
92. Prentice, "Widows Grieve," 4.
93. Ibid.
94. Petacque, "FBI Identifies 2 Men."
95. *USA v. Gargano, Raine, and Daniels*, 1968.

Chapter 3: October 28-29, 1967

96. Petacque and Casey, "Inside Story," 2.
97. Kenney, *Canton.*
98. *Canton Repository*, "'They Planned to Kill Us!'"
99. Ibid., 1.
100. Ibid.
101. Ibid.
102. *Marshall Evening Chronicle*, "Marshall Police Involved."
103. *Canton Repository*, "'They Planned to Kill Us!'" 1.
104. *Chicago Tribune*, "'Give up in Killing'" 1.
105. Shteir, *Striptease.*

106. Schmich, "606 Is Not Just a Park." According to local legend, the 606 Club gained local fame for visits from wealthy Democratic politicians and donors as its owner, Louis W. Nathan, was a Democratic precinct captain. Other interesting legends: the 606 Club was a frequent stop for attendees of the 1968 Democratic Convention, and the "606" in Chicago zip codes was in homage to the 606 Club.
107. Liebling, *Chicago*.
108. I have deliberately changed her name to protect her real identity.
109. Conner, "Confession," 12.
110. Ibid.
111. Ibid.
112. Daniels, Confession.
113. Conner, "Confession," 12.
114. Ibid.
115. Ibid.
116. Ibid.
117. Daniels, Confession.
118. Conner, "Confession," 12.
119. Ibid.
120. Ibid.
121. *Chicago Tribune*, "Doctor Denies Aid to Bandit," 1.
122. Ibid.
123. *Chicago Sun-Times*, "Was Offered $25,000 by Gang," 34.
124. Petacque, "Bank Robbery Serial Numbers," 5.
125. Taken from FBI interview of 606 Club manager, 91-HQ28365, Section 2, 1–5.
126. Petacque, "Bank Robbery Serial Numbers," 5.
127. J. Edgar Hoover initiated the FBI's identification database and fingerprinting system, which proved fruitful in clearly identifying these culprits.
128. Watson, "Hideaway at Lake Resort," 5–6.
129. Jackman, "Cabin Hideout," 2.
130. Watson, "Hideaway at Lake Resort," 5–6.
131. Ibid.
132. Ibid.
133. Ibid.

Chapter 4: October 30-31, 1967

134. *Chicago Tribune*, "Hunt Centered in Suburbs," 1.
135. Frailey, "Relatives Urge 2," 4.
136. *Chicago Tribune*, "Give Up in Killing," 1.
137. Ibid.
138. Frailey, "Relatives Urge 2," 4.
139. Ibid.
140. Ibid.
141. Ibid.
142. Ibid.
143. Talbott, "Policeman Who 'Loved People' Is Buried," 4.
144. *Chicago Tribune*, "400 at Last Rites," 2.
145. Gamboa Návar, *Northlake: Images of America*, 90.
146. Talbott, "Policeman Who 'Loved People' Is Buried," 16.
147. *Chicago Tribune*, "400 at Last Rites," 2.
148. Talbott, "Policeman Who 'Loved People' Is Buried," 4.
149. *Chicago Tribune*, "400 at Last Rites," 2.
150. Talbott, "Policeman Who 'Loved People' Is Buried," 4.
151. Ibid.
152. *Chicago Sun-Times*, "Tribute Paid," 2.
153. Ibid.
154. Petacque, "FBI Names 2," 42.
155. Ibid.
156. *Chicago Sun-Times*, "Gargano's Father Mourns Death."
157. *Daily Register*, "Armed Robbery."
158. FBI Investigation report, dated October 31, 1967, file # SI52-2478, 38.
159. Ibid., 40.
160. Ibid., 35.
161. FBI report IP 91-4832, October 31, 1967, 178.
162. Ibid.
163. *Chicago Tribune*, "2 Seized," 2.
164. FBI report IP 91-4832, October 31, 1967, 178.
165. Ibid.
166. Ibid.
167. Ibid., 197. Although a large quantity of money was retrieved, the Northlake Bank used decoy money, which probably included some of the bills found.
168. Ibid.

169. *Chicago Tribune*, "Two Women Also Nabbed," 1.
170. Ibid.
171. FBI Report 91-5607, 3.
172. Jonjack, "Before That," 5.
173. Enstad, "Link Bandits' Arsenal," 1.
174. Connor, "Accused Police Killers Charged," 2.
175. *Chicago Tribune*, "U.S. Indicts 3," 3.

Chapter 5: Legal Proceedings

176. *United States v. Jackson*. Precedent for this case came from a district court case in Connecticut argued in January 1967. Chief Judge Timbers ruled that that federal kidnapping statute's section that was applicable to the defendants' plea violated their Sixth Amendment right. The defendants' risk of death is greatly reduced if they waive their constitutional right to trial or plead guilty. In other words, they do not qualify for the death penalty since only a jury can recommend that punishment. The Northlake Bank robbers' lawyers decided because of this case to waive a jury trial. Yet national discussion carried this case to the Supreme Court, which ultimately decided against Judge Timbers's decision.
177. Hall, *Oxford Companion*, 1,069.
178. John, "Federal Defender Services."
179. According to Ronald Dale Raine's website article "Casing the Joint," "while awaiting trial, the judge, the U.S. Attorney, our lawyers, and the Marshalls all agreed that we would be getting the death penalty. J. Edgar Hoover's public debate with Myrl Alexander, the Director of Bureau Prisons, over our case, didn't improve our chances of escaping execution either. But then, *mirable dictu*, the Warren Supreme Court, so maligned and hated by the right-wingers, handed down the *Jackson* decision, effectively, ending the death penalty for such as us. However, since we had had experience with the 'federales,' knowing what awaited us, we weren't particularly overjoyed."
180. *United States Supreme Court Records*, 138.
181. Ibid.
182. Ibid.
183. Ibid., 141.
184. Ibid., 142.
185. Ibid.

186. Ibid.
187. Ibid., 146.
188. O'Brien, "Escape Foiled," 2.
189. Court Transcripts of Proceedings, United States District Court, Northern District of Illinois, Eastern Division, 5.
190. Ibid., 8.
191. Ibid.
192. Ibid.
193. Ibid., 9.
194. Ibid.
195. Ibid., 26.
196. Ibid.
197. Ibid., 30.
198. Ibid., 31.
199. Ibid., 34.
200. Ibid., 36.
201. Ibid.
202. Ibid., 37.
203. Ibid., 32.
204. Court Transcripts of Proceedings, United States District Court, Northern District of Illinois, Eastern Division.
205. Ibid.
206. *Daily Sububran Herald Chicago*, "Two Women Plead Guilty," 4.
207. *Chicago Tribune*, "Woman Gets Year," B6.
208. *Chicago Tribune*, "Woman, 42, Gets 4 Months," A11.

Epilogue

209. McManus, "Extremely Dangerous' Search," 1, 12.
210. Associated Press, "1 Marion Escapee," A2.
211. Gregory, "As a 78-year-old Cop Killer," 16.
212. *Mt. Vernon Register News*, "Marion Prison Inmate Writes Brief Guide." A "shank" is a knife; a "kite" is a note between inmates; a "fever" is an additional five-year term usually incurred because of fighting—all words commonly used during Gargano's prison term.
213. Taken from Ronald Dale Raine's website.
214. *Evansville Courier & Press*, Obituaries, September 3, 1999.

BIBLIOGRAPHY

Associated Press. "Defends U.S. Parole of 2 Bank Robbers, Chief of Board Tells Basis of Decisions." *Chicago Tribune*, November 3, 1967.

———. "1 Marion Escapee Remains at Large." *Lima News*, October 15, 1975.

Canton Repository. "'They Planned to Kill Us!' Says Nitzu." October 17, 1967.

Casey, James, and Jerry DeMuth. "Hunt Bank Killers of Two Cops." *Chicago Sun-Times*, October 28, 1967.

Chicago Daily Tribune. "Father Cited After His Son Admits Theft." March 23, 1946.

———. "136 lbs. Butter, Burglars' Loot, Goes Back Home." March 12, 1946.

———. "Sgt. Pat Sends Butter He Can't Eat to Cooler." March 11, 1946.

Chicago Sun-Times. "FBI Chief Raps Parole Setup, Cites Northlake Case." November 2, 1967.

———. "Gargano's Father Mourns Death." November 4, 1967.

———. "Northlake Hunt Yields Weapons, 'Hit Car.'" November 4, 1967.

———. "Tribute Paid to 2nd Slain Cop." November 1, 1967.

———. "Was Offered $25,000 by Gang, Doctor Says." November 2, 1967.

Chicago Tribune. "Capture 2 in Cop Killings." November 1, 1967.

———. "Doctor Denies Aid to Bandit." November 2, 1967.

———. "400 at Last Rites Pay Tribute to Slain Northlake Policeman." October 31, 1967.

———. "Four Suspects in Bank Crime Returned Here." November 4, 1967.

———. "Gargano Says He's Innocent of Cop Killing." December 13, 1967.

———. "Give Up in Killing, Dad Begs." October 31, 1967.

———. "Hunt Centered in Suburbs for Killers." October 30, 1967.

———. "3 Grand Jury Trial." June 7, 1968.

———. "U.S. Indicts 3 in Robbery, Cop Killings." November 3, 1967.

———. "Woman, 42, Gets 4 Months for Aiding Killer." January 16, 1969.

———. "Woman Gets Year for Helping Killers." January 9, 1968.

Connor, Monica Florence. "Confession." IP 91-4832, 1967.

Connor, Thomas. "Accused Police Killers Charged." *Chicago Tribune*, November 2, 1967.

Court Transcripts of Proceedings, United States District Court, Northern District of Illinois, Eastern Division.

Daily Register. "Armed Robbery at Kroger Saturday." September 11, 1967.

———. "Sheriff Reports Finding Car Stolen by Kroger Burglars." September 19, 1967.

Daily Suburban Herald Chicago. "Two Women Plead Guilty; End of Bank Robbery Saga." November 20, 1968.

Daniels, Clifton Orneal. Confession. LaPorte, Indiana, October 31, 1967.

Drummond, John. "Officer: No Parole for '67 Cop Killer." CBS 2 Chicago. October 20, 2010.

Enstad, Robert. "Link Bandits' Arsenal to Armory Robbery." *Chicago Tribune*, November 2, 1967.

Enterprise. "Robbery at Parks Bros." July 1967.

Evansville Courier & Press. Obituaries. September 3, 1999.

FBI Archives 1244059-0 001 HQ 101 60, FBI Graduation, November 2, 1967.

FBI Report of the Identification Division. FBI File No. 91-28365, Latent Case No. 85126, December 19, 1967.

Federal Bureau of Investigation. "A Brief History of the FBI." http://www.fbi.gov/about-us/history/brief-history/brief-history.

Fisher, Dennis. "Slayers Believed Still in Suburbs." *Chicago Sun-Times*, October 30, 1967.

Frailey, Fred. "Relatives Urge 2: Give Up!" *Chicago Sun-Times*, October 31, 1967.

Fulwood, Isaac. "History of the Federal Parole System." U.S. Department of Justice, May 2003. www.justice.gov/sites/default/files/uspc/legacy/2009/10/07/history.pdf.

Gamboa Návar, Edgar. *Northlake: Images of Americ*a. Charleston, SC: Arcadia Publishing, 2012.

Granger, William. "Services Are Set for Slain Policemen." *Chicago Tribune*, October 30, 1967.

Gregory, Ted. "As a 78-year-old Cop Killer Faces Parole Hearing, System Faces Costs of Elderly Prisoners." *Chicago Tribune*, December 4, 2010.

BIBLIOGRAPHY

Gregory, Ted, and Dan Hinkel. "After 43 Years, Cop Killer Set to Walk Free." *Chicago Tribune*, July 14, 2010.

Grossman, James R., Ann Durkin Keating and Janice L. Reiff. *Encyclopedia of Chicago*. Chicago: University of Chicago Press, 2004.

Hall, Kermit L. *The Oxford Companion to the Supreme Court of the United States.* New York: Oxford University Press, 2005.

Jackman, Arthur. "Cabin Hideout Not Exactly a Luxury One." *Chicago Tribune*, November 2, 1967.

John, J. Cleary. "Federal Defender Services: Serving the System or the Client?" *Law and Contemporary Problems* 58, no. 1 (Winter 1995).

Joliet Herald-News. "Gunmen Rob, Beat Restaurant Owner." September 5, 1967.

Jonjack, Donald. "Before That, It's a Bellwood Flat." *Chicago Sun-Times.* November 1, 1967.

Kearns, Jerry. "Pathological Report and Protocol." 1967.

Kenney, Kimberly A. *Canton: A Journey Through Time*. Charleston, SC: Arcadia Publishing, 2003.

Liebling, Joseph Abbott. *Chicago: The Second City*. New York: Knopf Publishers, 1952.

Malby, Andy. "Willow Creek Boy Turned Cop Killer Dies in Prison." *Three Forks Herald*, March 20, 2013.

Marshall Evening Chronicle. "Marshall Police Involved in Wild Chase with Bandits." October 14, 1967.

McManus, Ed. "'Extremely Dangerous' Search for 5 Convicts." *Chicago Tribune*, October 12, 1975.

Montgomery, Dennis. "Marion Prison Inmate Writes Brief Guide to Slang." *Mt. Vernon Register News*, March 31, 1976.

Mt. Vernon Register News. "Marion Prison Inmate Writes Brief Guide to Prison Slang." March 31, 1976.

O'Brien, John. "Escape Foiled; 3 Cop Killers Get 199 Years." *Chicago Tribune*, July 17, 1968.

———. "3 Cop Killers Get 199 Years." *Chicago Tribune*, July 17, 1968.

Petacque, Art. "Bank Robbery Serial Numbers Recorded." *Chicago Sun-Times*, October 31, 1967.

———. "FBI Identifies 2 Men Sought in Northlake Bank Holdup, Killings." *Chicago Sun-Times*, October 29, 1967.

———. "Northlake Bank Holdup Suspects Quickly Indicted." *Chicago Sun-Times*, November 3, 1967.

Petacque, Art, and James Casey. "Inside Story of Suspect's Arrest." *Chicago Sun-Times*, November 2, 1967.

Prentice, Abra. "Widows Grieve, Tell Happy Lives." C*hicago Sun-Times*. October 28, 1967.

Raine, Ronald Dale. "Casing the Joint." www.oocities.org/standingdeer1/delraine3.htm.

Schmich, Mary. "606 Is Not Just a Park, but a Strip Club Legend." *Chicago Tribune*. June 16, 2015.

Shteir, Rachel. *Striptease: The Untold History of the Girlie Show*. New York: Oxford University Press, 2004.

Sonderby, Max. "FBI Displays Bandit Gang's Deadly Firepower Arsenal." *Chicago Sun-Times*, November 2, 1967.

Sonderby, Max, and James Casey. "All Robbery Suspects Under Guard Held." *Chicago Sun-Times*, November 4, 1967.

Stumer, William Q. "Pathological Report and Protocol." 1967.

Talbott, Basil, Jr. "Policemen Who 'Loved People' Is Buried." *Chicago Sun-Times*, October 31, 1967.

Thomson, John R. "Bank Holdup Manhunt Recalls Dillinger Era." *Chicago Tribune*, November 5, 1967.

———. "How Violence Built Up to a Climax." *Chicago Tribune*, November 2, 1967.

United States Supreme Court Records: October Term, 1967, Lawyer's Edition. Rochester, NY: Lawyers Cooperative Publishing Company, 1969.

United States v. Jackson, 262 F.Supp. 716 (D. Conn. 1967). Filed January 9, 1967. https://www.courtlistener.com/opinion/2351390/united-states-v-jackson.

USA v. Henry Michael Gargano, Ronald Dale Raine, and Clifton Orneal Daniels. Northern District of Illinois, Eastern Division, 1968.

Watson, Jerome. "Hideaway at Lake Resort Is Fugitives' Last Stop." *Chicago Sun-Times*, November 1, 1967.

———. "10:41 A.M., an Alarm—Then Death at the Bank." *Chicago Sun-Times*, October 28, 1967.

Whisler, Weldon. "Nation-wide Alert Ordered for Slayers of 2 Policemen," *Chicago Tribune*, October 28, 1967.

Wolf, Sheila. "Policemen's Wives Tell of Worrying." *Chicago Tribune*, October 28, 1967.

INDEX

ABOUT THE AUTHOR

After living in Chicago for the first ten years of his life, Edgar Gamboa Návar moved to suburban Northlake, just outside Chicago, in 1985. Although he was apprehensive at first about the move, Northlake became a great city to live in and spend his adolescent years. He quickly integrated himself to life in Northlake by participating in its most popular sport at the time: baseball. Beyond sports, Edgar has enjoyed learning about Northlake's past, especially the Northlake Bank robbery that captured the region's attention.

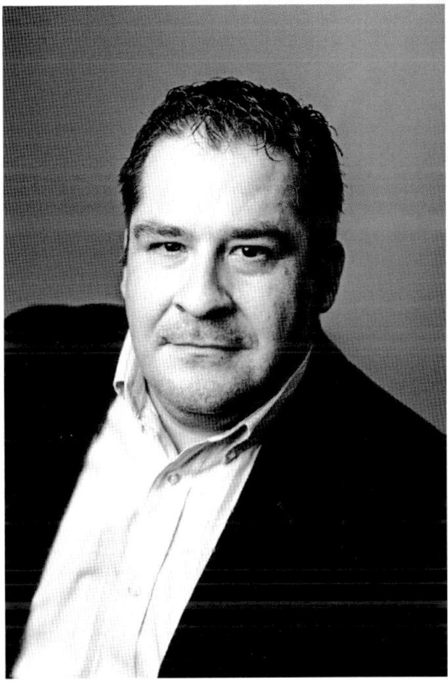